NEWBOURNE IN SHORT TROUSERS

LEIGH BELCHAM

To my brothers, Michael and Jeremy, who grew up with me in the 1940s and 1950s, and to the memory of our parents, Neville and Dorrie, who worked hard to do what was right and trusted us to do the same.

Half-pint Publishing

First published 2014
Half-pint publishing
45a Western Avenue
Felixstowe IP11 9SL
01394 285674
halfpintpublish@aol.com

ISBN 978-0-9930746-0-8

All profits on the sale of this book will be donated to

> The Museum of English Rural Life
> University of Reading
> Redlands Road
> Reading RG1 5EX

Cover design: Adrian Belcham and Ron Waltham
Printed in Great Britain by EAM Printers, Ipswich

PREFACE

Three strokes of a pen. That was all it took to change the village of Newbourne for ever.

George Denn Turner's signature on October 20th 1936 confirmed the sale of his home, Newbourne Hall, and nearly 500 acres of agricultural land to the Land Settlement Association.

The 80 or so villagers were quite unprepared. Their unspoilt and picturesque Suffolk valley between Ipswich, Woodbridge and Felixstowe, only accessible by single-track roads, was to undergo rapid and radical change.

During the next three years, nearly fifty smallholdings and several Association staff houses were added to Newbourne's handful of cottages and farms, church and chapel, pub, shop and post office. Farm buildings surrounding Newbourne Hall became offices, stores and a packing shed. Hedges were grubbed up and a concrete road built to serve the far reaches of the development.

The LSA's Newbourne Estate was one of several such schemes providing work for long-term unemployed men from parts of the country affected by the economic downturn of the 1930s. In early 1937, Newbourne's residents, most of whom had been born and raised in the area, were confronted by the first of the newcomers. Within three years the village's population had more than doubled as a veritable tide of these men and their families arrived, most from the industrial north-east.

When war broke out in 1939, the focus of recruitment had to be changed. The association began to target men with agricultural experience and a limited amount of capital. As a consequence, my father, Neville Belcham, took on the tenancy of a smallholding in Newbourne in 1942: 47 Jackson Road.

I was two-and-a-half, and for the next 16 years lived with my parents and two younger brothers at the far end of that narrow concrete road. To start with, we had no car or telephone, and had to tramp half a mile along a muddy track to the nearest bus stop. Primary school was nearly a mile away across fields. Getting to and from the village centre and estate office involved a two-mile walk or cycle ride.

This book could justifiably be called *Growing up in Newbourne in the 'forties and 'fifties*. Our lives in this rural backwater might be hard to imagine for children of the iPad generation. How did our parents cope with the deprivations and uncertainties of war? How did we as children manage without television, sex education, smart phones or long trousers? They will certainly envy us the minimal parental supervision we enjoyed!

Stories of other, older children are included. Their parents were the very first settlers in 1937 and 1938 – the Madgwicks, Vickerstaffs, Samples, Cheshers, Grattons, Hedleys and Lockes. Some recall the tensions – and sometimes the fisticuffs – between the established population of "duzzy Suffolkers" and the incoming unemployed Geordies. Newbourne's local, The Fox, together with the church, chapel, community hut and school, played its part in breaking down barriers and fostering a welcome community spirit.

Newbourne in short trousers is in many respects a piece of social history. It describes life in an idyllic setting subjected to sudden and dramatic change. Family and working life were hard to separate for those living at the sharp end of this bold social experiment. Both were affected by the decisions of a seemingly remote officialdom in London and, in the early days, the threat and reality of war. Differences in family background and aspiration were not always well handled.

Although interesting in their own right, the stories and events in this book took place in the wider context of the LSA's local and national operation. This may be unfamiliar to many readers, so I have tried to weave some of this history into the stories themselves. I have a feeling that even Newbourne residents of long standing may learn something fresh about life in their village all those years ago. Certainly, I did!

"I've often wondered that," may be a common response to some nugget mined from musty and long-forgotten archives. How did Jackson Road get its name? What is or are puddingpokes? Why were smallholdings 40 to 43 numbered out of sequence? Which smallholding was also the Post Office?

But it is the personal anecdotes of those of us now in our *"twilight years"*, as my son insists on calling them, which form the bulk of this book. Memories of war, rationing, searchlights, our own "Dad's Army", and US airmen baling out over Newbourne. Our school days, with canings by the headmistress, Miss Cain (honestly!), and seeing who could pee highest on the school urinal roof. Elder-wood pop guns with acorns as ammunition, rodeos with pigs instead of horses, and rescuing chickens by boat in the 1953 east coast floods. And accidents and injuries too numerous to mention, with scars remaining to this day.

Anyone wanting a more straightforward historical narrative will find an appendix covering the rise and demise of the Land Settlement Association as a national organisation, as well as its Newbourne estate. Just before its official winding up in early 1983, the LSA was described in parliament as *"the largest producer of salad crops in Britain."* Clearly, some things had gone well. But working in what one tenant characterised as a *"compulsory co-operative"* also involved many trials and frustrations. The effects of these were felt well into the 1990s, and ultimately involved the government in a £6.5 million out-of-court settlement with former tenants. Clearly, other things had gone badly.

It has taken me about two years to write this book, two years that I have found immensely interesting and enjoyable. I hope that those who read it, whether they experienced Newbourne in short trousers or are just intrigued to hear about those who did, will enjoy it, too.

Leigh Belcham   *Felixstowe, November 2014*

ABOUT THE AUTHOR

After an engineering apprenticeship in Coventry, Leigh changed direction. Two further years at college were followed by twelve in professional youth work in inner-city Birmingham and rural Cambridgeshire. From 1976 to 2002 he was engaged in the management of Christian residential youth activities, both in the UK and overseas. In 2002 Leigh returned to Suffolk with his wife, Jill. They have two sons, are now retired and live in Felixstowe.

ACKNOWLEDGEMENTS

M any have contributed to this book, sharing their memories, trawling through photo albums, and introducing me to others prepared to do likewise. There has been much laughter as well as a little sadness on the way. Without their involvement, a better title would have been *Newbourne in short.*

I am particularly grateful to Wally Hammond, a close friend of my father, for writing the Foreword; to Sue Whittaker for allowing me to quote extensively from the manuscript of her late father's unpublished book, *Swords into Ploughshares and back;* and to the staff of the Museum of English Rural Life at Reading University, which holds the LSA's national archive. MERL will receive any profits from sales of this book.

Staff of the Suffolk Record Office in Ipswich have been most helpful. They hold early records of the LSA's Newbourne Estate, deposited by John Somerville of Newbourne Hall and used with his permission. John has been a wise advisor throughout.

I am pleased that Jeanne Gilder, who worked with my father for many years, was willing to rack her brains on many occasions, even if this was only on condition she was mentioned in the book. *"At last I'll be famous,"* she said, *"even if I've had to wait till I'm nearly 90!"* Ivy Griffiths and Georgie Madgwick were similarly obliging, with memories of their families' arrival from the north-east in 1937 and 1939.

Thanks are due to EAM Printers in Ipswich for permission to reproduce photos and text from Walter Tye's article, *The Newbourn Settlement,* in the *East Anglian Magazine,* March 1961; to Clifford Abbott, who lent files from his late father, Walter; to Professor Paul Hadley and the LSA Charitable Trust for permission to use photos from *An experiment in smallholdings*; to John Smith for permission to include photos from *Village life in and around Felixstowe*; and IPC Media for allowing reproduction of photos from *The Field.*

Many others, including my brothers, Michael and Jeremy, have kindly provided stories, photos and information. These are duly acknowledged on the relevant pages. I am very grateful to them, as well as to John Bale, Elizabeth Christman, John Cole, Bob Crawley, Michael Frost, Val Hill, Stella James, Marina O'Connell, Roger Salter, David Sterry, Pauline Stone, Alyson Videlo, and Peter and Sue Waller.

Last, but by no means least, I want to thank my wife, Jill, for patiently playing second fiddle to Newbourne for two years, and for her as-ever invaluable proof-reading and suggestions. Our two sons kindly used their professional skills – Richard in editing the text and Adrian, working with colleague Ron Waltham, in designing the cover. I am immensely grateful to them.

If names have been missed, it is entirely unintentional and I can only apologise. Corrections will gladly be made in any future editions.

OTHER SOURCES

Land settlers go back to slum homes, Cairns Post, July 5th 1938

Unemployed! Industrial transfers, Picture Post, February 11th 1939

From dole to farm, The Times, May 8th 1939

The Newbourn Estate, The Field, Ralph Whitlock, June 14th 1947

An experiment in smallholdings, Land Settlement Association, ca 1949

Farming costs shared, The Field, Ralph Whitlock, April 17th 1958

The Newbourn Settlement, The East Anglian Magazine, Walter Tye, March 1961

The Land Settlement Association – Its History and Present Form K J McCready. Occasional Paper 37, Plunkett Foundation, 1974.

Time-proven, but adaptable, Country Life, Sept 10th 1981

Hansard, 20th December 1982: Stanley Newens, MP for Harlow

Swords into ploughshares and back, manuscript of an unpublished book by Richard "Dick" Whittaker, 1984, used by kind permission of his daughter, Sue Whittaker.

Village life in and around Felixstowe, Smith, Wylie, White & Hadwen, 2003

The Land Settlement Association Ltd, 1934 – 1983: An epilogue, Philip G Hamlett, 2005

'Go home, you miners!': Fen Drayton and the LSA, Pamela Dearlove, 2007 (£8.95 from Pamela at redtiles@mac.com)

The Land Settlement Association (LSA): Its co-operative ideals and their implementation, Peter Clarke, Northampton Sq, *2012*

Other press reports and conversations are acknowledged within the text. This list of sources is also included at the end of Appendix D – *The Land Settlement Association: its rise and demise.*

FOREWORD

by Wally Hammond, grower in Newbourne from 1952 to 2008

Thank goodness I had left my wife and 9-week old son to follow at the end of the week! Our new smallholding, 22 Mill Road in Newbourne, had no electricity, and Arthur Gilder, the estate handyman, was still painting the kitchen.

13th October 1952 was a very wet day. My father and I had brought our coal ration in the back of the furniture van, so we were able to light a fire in the kitchen range to cook some food. Once the van had left, Beryl Whittaker arrived to say that Dick had contacted the electricity board to get the power restored the next day. She also invited us both to their home at No. 23 opposite for a meal.

This was the first of many acts of kindness Sheila and I were to receive during our 56 years in Newbourne. Dick and Beryl remained friends throughout, with their children and ours growing up together.

During the next few years I tried to understand just how the Land Settlement Association worked in practice, and it was then that I met Neville and Dorrie Belcham. Neville and I travelled to Swanwick in Derbyshire to a conference of the LSA and the National Association of LSA Tenants (NALSAT). We were representing the Newbourne tenants. I learned nothing of importance at the conference except that LSA staff and tenants seemed to be on a collision course over most things.

However, I did get to know Neville much better, and realised we had similar ideas about growing and wanting to improve the way we worked. Neville already had ten years' experience of working with the LSA, and knew what would and would not be profitable to grow under the scheme.

One evening after they had finished harvesting their spring lettuce crop, Neville and Dorrie invited Sheila and me to supper. We were just starting to cut our lettuce. We had an extremely pleasant evening, but I gradually realised that their money was already in the bank and I was way behind. We agreed to work together to try to help each other along the road to becoming better growers.

About this time I introduced Neville to my wife's father, Mr R E Frampton from Chichester. He used his influence as a director of Efford Horticultural Research Station to persuade our local ADAS

Horticultural Officer, Terry Kingsley, to set up a tomato study group similar to one running in West Sussex. Neville became chairman and Terry Kingsley secretary. The group, which included growers from Newbourne, Kirton, Clacton, Capel, Kesgrave and Leiston, ran very successfully for about four years and really raised our standard of growing.

I lost a great friend when Neville died. We didn't mix socially – his great love was sailing, mine music – but it didn't stop us seeing each other regularly.

Imagine my surprise when a couple arrived at No.22 one day about ten years ago. *"Does Wally Hammond still live here?"* they asked. I didn't have to ask the man's name. If he'd had a pipe in his mouth, I'd have said, *"Hello, Neville."* It was Leigh and Jill Belcham. I hadn't known the Belcham boys as youngsters as they lived much of their life away from the village, but I was always kept up-to-date with their doings.

When Leigh decided to write about his parents and growing up in Newbourne, I was delighted. I have learned a lot more about Neville and Dorrie, as well as about Newbourne before, during and after the war. And his research on the LSA has been meticulous.

This book will commend itself to anyone interested in what happens when a village is invaded and rebuilt as it was in the 1930s. The LSA had a major impact on the area. But it needs to be remembered that the impact was no less dramatic when the scheme folded in 1983.

Leigh has researched and recorded all the facts, and is to be congratulated on this piece of social history. I know – I lived through it all.

Newbourne in the mid-1930s

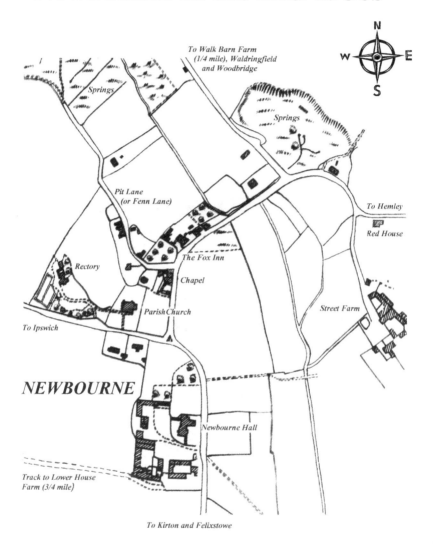

(Based on a map in the Land Settlement Association archives in the Museum of English Rural Life at Reading University)

Newbourne in the mid-1940s

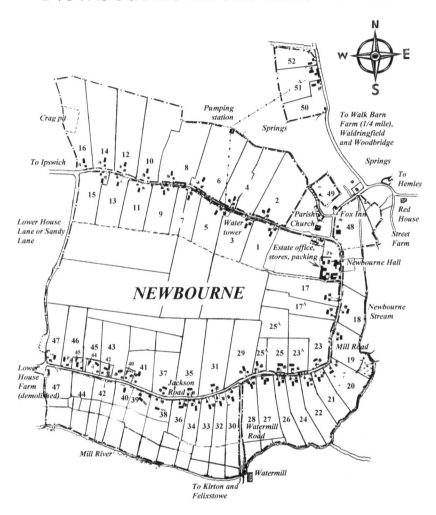

(Based on maps in the Land Settlement Association archives in the Museum of English Rural Life at Reading University)

NEWBOURNE
IN SHORT TROUSERS

CONTENTS

1 – DOWN SANDY LANE

He had cycled down Sandy Lane twice during the previous four months. But my father really should have known better than to drive down it in a car, least of all one he had hired.

Sandy Lane in Newbourne is officially Lower House Lane. Nowadays it is a gated, private driveway serving the modern chalet bungalow and surrounding meadowland called Lower House Farm. But throughout the 25 years we lived at its junction with Jackson Road, it was half-a-mile of narrow, rutted track, with tussocks of grass and large puddles. It was also the shortest route from the village outskirts on Ipswich Road to our home. The alternative was three times as long, even though it was on tarmac and concrete.

It was late morning on Tuesday 1st December 1942 when my father decided to take the scenic route. We turned into the lane from Ipswich Road, and began the increasingly bumpy drive down into the wooded valley and to our new home on smallholding number 47. Here

my two brothers and I would spend our childhood and teenage years, with Sandy Lane playing a large part in our lives. At its lower end, an accumulation of fine sand washed from the light Suffolk soil of surrounding fields gave it its name. It also served as a marvellous skid-pan – and cushion – for us youngsters careering

Sandy Lane: author (L) and Michael, 1944

down the final few yards of this, our very own cycle track.

That morning we had travelled from the Land Settlement Association's Foxash estate at Lawford in Essex, where we had been living on another smallholding since June 1940. I was only two-and-a-half, but can still remember sitting in the front passenger seat, with my mother and two-month-old Michael in the back. Our younger brother Jeremy wouldn't be born till 1946, so he missed it altogether.

The day had dawned bright and frosty. The oaks and elms on each

13

side had shed the last of their leaves, allowing the wintry sun to penetrate what in summer would have been a dense, green canopy. But my father's focus during this final leg of the journey was less on the scenery than on safely negotiating sundry hazards. Not least of these were the overhanging branches threatening the car's bodywork. My mother recalled her own feelings on paper many years later:

"I shall never forget the sight of the Dutch Mansard roof through the trees, and the valley and meadow and streams and woods beyond! It seemed like heaven! Ten acres, and orchard and all."

The two years at Foxash had not been easy for my parents. The war was a major factor, of course. The German Luftwaffe's targets of the port at Manningtree and British Xylonite's works at Brantham were too close for comfort. They had never been happy there, in what my mother described as *"an unloved and inconvenient cottage."* My father – Neville – was not very well, and was always looking about for something better.

In summer 1942 he learned of a larger, vacant LSA holding at Newbourne, and had set off immediately to find out more. My mother – Doreen, but usually known as Dorrie – was eight months pregnant, so he travelled alone, taking his bicycle on the train from Manningtree to Ipswich. He clearly liked what he saw, and took photos to show my mother on his return. Sadly, she never had the opportunity to view them as he left his camera on Ipswich station in the blackout!

Even without the photos, it was not difficult to convince my mother that the move would be sensible. But the next few months were far from easy. As she later recalled, *"Michael was born, Neville had pneumonia, and I had my hands full. Also, we were dive-bombed almost every day or night, especially when foggy."*

So we arrived in Newbourne. The removal van was delayed, so milk was heated on the stove for Michael and me. Our parents enjoyed a tray of tea and a competition-standard sponge cake brought by Ethel Pettitt from number 45. Ethel was a rather short lady with badly bowed legs, who seemed never to be without her apron. Her husband Fred was responsible for the estate's horses, some of which were kept on the field across the road from their house. They were wonderful neighbours for many years, even after they moved to Elesay Cottages opposite the church. It was there that we watched our first television programme, which I recall looked more like a snowstorm!

We were very fortunate to have one of the smallholdings with a four-bedroomed house. The standard house on Newbourne estate had three bedrooms and a simple gable roof. Those with four bedrooms had the distinctive hipped gambrel roof, better – but apparently inaccurately – known, as the Dutch Mansard.

These larger houses had a separate bathroom with WC, while the smaller ones had their baths curtained off in an alcove in the kitchen. Georgie Madgwick's parents had one of these smaller houses at 19 Mill Road from early 1939. Georgie remembers some of the original tenants preferring to keep coal in the bath, and maintain their tradition of bathing in a galvanised tub in front of the living room

47 Jackson Road, 1943

range. Since front doors were only used by strangers, and back doors opened directly into the kitchen, this practice did reduce the potential for embarrassing moments.

Sometime in the 1960s, the smaller houses were extended by adding a separate bathroom and additional room on the ground floor. However, even these houses as originally built offered unimagined luxury to some of the early occupants. On February 11th 1939, *Picture Post* magazine featured Nathan Turner, an unemployed Durham miner, who had been accepted as a tenant on another of the

One of the smaller houses
(East Anglian Magazine)

LSA's estates at Caversham, near Reading. Nathan, 54, had worked for only 36 weeks in the previous fourteen and a half years. For 21 years he had lived with his wife and up to six children *"in one dank bedroom and a kitchen"*. For him, a new three-bedroomed detached home in the countryside will have been a palace.

To my parents, too, our new home must have seemed

like a palace. That morning they had left a semi-detached, *"unloved and inconvenient cottage"* at Foxash, with German bombers an ever-present reality. As they looked around our new home, and took in the surroundings, they must have felt as if a new life was beginning.

But life can be tough, even in palaces, as they were soon to discover.

Jackson Road in 1946, with No. 47 in background (The Field)

16

2 – MEADOWS, STREAMS AND WOODS

As children, we were oblivious to the war and other adult concerns. Our new surroundings were idyllic, and we lost no time in exploring everything that our end of the estate had to offer. Our parents enjoyed it all with us, but soon we were venturing forth on our own. The main attraction, inevitably, was the crystal-clear Mill River meandering quietly through the valley only a few hundred yards from our house. The *"big stream"*, as it was always known, and its *"big bridge"*, saw many an enactment of Winnie-the-Pooh's game of

"Poohsticks" on the big bridge (author and Michael)

Poohsticks. Today the bridge is much smaller, with a larger bridge about 100 yards farther downstream, where the water can be seen in the background in the photograph.

Fallen branches from the overhanging trees would create pools of slow-moving water, harbouring creepy-crawlies and small fish. The water meadows adjacent were full of wild flowers in summer, with kingcups and meadowsweet close to the stream. A narrower water course – the *"little stream"*, naturally – was nearer to our house, and

17

had a small population of stickleback and abundant watercress. Between the little stream and Jackson Road was a much drier meadow on slightly higher ground, full of ragwort and cow pats.

Immediately beyond the big stream was a piece of poorly-managed woodland. This was part of what is shown on older maps as Great Grove. Some of this was carpeted with primroses in the spring, bluebells in early summer, and spent 12-bore cartridges during autumn and winter. A narrow, sandy brook wound its way towards the big stream between coppiced hazel trees, the uniformly straight shoots of which would in later years be converted into bows and arrows.

These meadows, streams and woods were reached from our house by a short track leading southwards from the end of Jackson Road. To the left of what is now only a gated footpath, bordered incongruously by eucalyptus and other shrubs and trees more appropriate in a park or garden, were the remains of an old barn. This was about fifty yards from the road and had been part of what was originally Lower Farm. It is shown clearly on several old maps, including a survey done in 1804. The barn had been demolished a few years after the LSA arrived, and my mother used the remaining bricks to construct a horseshoe-shaped

The sundial with Tudor bricks in 1944: author with parents and Michael.

sunken rose garden with a sundial at its centre. The size and shape of the bricks appear consistent with my parents' conviction that the barn was of Tudor origin.

On the opposite side of the track, where the detached chalet bungalow now stands, were the remains of the former Lower House. Census and other records show this to have been two semi-detached cottages. Until late 1937, these had been in continuous occupation since at least the early 19th Century, housing men all described as agricultural labourers, together with their families.

In 1938 the cottages were recorded as derelict. Their abandoned gardens – or orchard, as we knew them – with fruit trees and a well, were quickly overrun by nettles and brambles, but later became a wonderful playground for us local children. Bramley, Russet, and Tom

18

Putt apples and Victoria plums abounded, and were a welcome supplement to wartime diets. Daffodils and violets, including a white variety, enhanced the bouquets of primroses gathered from the wood each Mothering Sunday. A holly tree, which sadly never seemed to have berries, was a boon at Christmas. Jim Wicks, now living at No. 40 Jackson Road, remembers as a child finding birds' nests in the footings of the demolished cottages. And no, no-one to my knowledge ever fell down the well!

Our house was separated from Sandy Lane by a thick, tall hedge that seemed to consist mainly of brambles. The inevitable scratches were somehow made more bearable by bumper crops of blackberries, especially when baked in pies with Bramley apples from the orchard. A few yards farther up the lane were two abandoned crag pits, one on each side. Both doubtless featured in the coprolite extraction industry* of the mid-19th Century, when these *"phosphatic nodules"* – reckoned by some to be fossilised dinosaur dung – were dug from seams of crag for sale to fertiliser manufacturers. The crag itself had long been recognised for its fertilising qualities, but I suspect this fact may have escaped my parents. They used it liberally to surface our garden paths, and must have despaired as the weeds on the paths grew faster than the flowers in the beds!

The smaller of the two pits would later serve as a safe location for our fireworks and bonfire each November. Sand martins used holes in the crag for their nests. But the larger pit had far more to offer adventurous children. It had been used to dump the trunks of several large, mature trees, which I guess had been felled during the construction of Jackson Road. The origin of a considerable quantity of broken glass was anyone's guess. It was down the precipitous cliff along the field edge that we were several years later to roll my brother, Michael, in a 40-gallon oil drum. The large oak he hit on the way down is still there.

All in all, a wonderful place to grow up. But as a place of work, it was not ideal – at least to start with.

For much more about Newbourne and the coprolite extraction industry, visit www.bernardoconnor.org.uk/Coprolites/Suffcops/NEWBOURN.htm

3 - "AN ODD SORT OF HOLDING"

We were not the first occupants of 47 Jackson Road. The first was Harold Smith, a pigman, who moved there from Oak Cottage near Kembroke Hall. Harold arrived in either autumn 1937 or spring 1938, depending on which of the LSA's records you choose to believe. From then until sometime in late 1939 or early 1940 it was used for breeding pigs for the rest of the estate. The first tenant at No. 47, Jack Russell, came in March 1940 and left just before our arrival in December 1942.

At that time the ten-acre smallholding was one of the largest on the estate. Much hard graft would be needed, especially when we three children had grown into hungry, high-maintenance teenagers. The previous two years at Foxash on a much smaller holding had given my father valuable experience, but it would still be a steep learning curve. A seven-year apprenticeship in London in the printing industry, and four years using those skills with newspapers in Fleet Street, would not be a great help. Assessing the pros and cons of growing tomatoes outdoors or how to prevent chickens pecking each other required other expertise.

I have often wondered how a man with no apparent agricultural experience or training could have been granted the tenancy of a smallholding. He had begun his apprenticeship in 1929 only a few months after leaving school in Southend. Soon after completing his training in 1936, he appears to have started work in Fleet Street. In 1937 he and my mother married and settled in Orpington in Kent, better described as a London suburb than somewhere known for its high unemployment or agriculture.

Yet the LSA did accept him as a tenant. He left suburbia and the city, and, after two years at Foxash, ran the smallholding in Newbourne for 25 years. During that time he successfully supported himself, his wife and three sons, and played a prominent role in several key developments in tomato and lettuce production on the estate. When he died of cancer in 1967, aged only 54, the LSA advertised the holding – I think in *The Grower*. I recently learned that this was the first time they had felt justified in advertising a smallholding, at least in Newbourne, as a worthwhile going concern.

The determining factor in his acceptance by the LSA was almost certainly the declaration of war in September 1939. The Association's 21 estates had been established during the mid- to late 1930s. They were to provide work for long-term unemployed men from the government-designated Special Areas such as the industrial north-east. Recruitment fluctuated during the first few years, but by May 1939, according to a Head Office memo, Newbourne estate was fully occupied. However, the onset of war meant that many of these men signed up for the armed services or found ready employment in factories. Several who had already undergone training with the LSA

were keen to fight for their country, and some had left. Those remaining had to be reminded that agricultural work was a Reserved Occupation, an essential part of the war effort. Government grants were withdrawn, and the LSA began recruiting men with agricultural experience and a limited amount of capital. The continued development of these small-holdings was obviously vital, not only because of money already invested but because food imports were severely curtailed.

My parents pre-LSA

My father was somehow able to raise the required capital of £300. I recall mention of his borrowing £50 from his mother, which he presumably added to whatever equity he and my mother had in their bungalow in Orpington. In any case, the LSA's concern that all holdings were occupied and productive meant that bank loans were often available to meet any shortfall.

But how did he convince the LSA he had the necessary agricultural knowledge and experience?

Archive records show that his own father, Edmund, had been variously a farmer and dairyman, a job master, a cab proprietor and a fruiterer, all in Southend, Essex. But Edmund had died in 1926 when my father was only 13, so any associated know-how and experience would hardly have rubbed off on his son. I find it hard to believe this would have met the LSA's requirement of agricultural experience.

Perhaps I shall never know for sure. Nevertheless, here we were at the end of 1942 on what was described in an LSA Head Office memo three-and-a-half years earlier as *"an odd sort of holding"*.

Until 1939, this had consisted of seven acres of land on the north side of Jackson Road, together with a glasshouse and a 6-sty piggery. Some pigs were also kept on the opposite side of the road in the barn that was soon to be demolished.

The memo described the land at No. 47 as *"thin and somewhat hilly"*, and *"obviously unsuited to intensive horticultural development"*. With other holdings fully occupied, it was decided to develop No. 47 as another tenanted smallholding, but with a pig bias. However, the seven acres were deemed *"hardly sufficient for 15 to 20 sows"*, so a decision was made to add a further eight acres by including the two fields on the opposite side of the road. Since these belonged to holding No. 46, between three and four acres were to be taken from No. 47's land on the north side of the road and given to No. 46 in exchange.

The LSA envisaged an incoming tenant with experience of pigs or who at least showed some aptitude for them. They didn't seem to be in any immediate hurry to make the changes, but the declaration of war only three months later introduced two factors that may have forced a re-think. Importing feeding stuff for pigs became both difficult and dangerous, so the costs of keeping stock increased significantly. The same dangers and difficulties also made it important for the country to become self-sufficient in feeding its human population.

Harold Smith left at some point during the next twelve months. Jack Russell moved in in March 1940. A Hampshire farmer's son, he had been with his father on a 500-acre farm for 20 years. The rent of the holding was £45 0s 0d, and the incoming valuation £63 4s 3d. By this time, the two fields on the opposite side of the road had been incorporated, offset by a reduction in acreage on the north side in favour of No. 46. A battery house for poultry had also been added, backing on to Sandy Lane, probably in early 1940.

Two years later, Jack Russell gave notice to quit. He apparently felt that the holding, devoted mainly to stock, was never likely to produce a satisfactory income in what were increasingly difficult times. He left shortly before we arrived on 1st December that year.

Soon after our arrival, my parents borrowed the name *Lower House* for No. 47. They reluctantly returned it to John Anderson when he built his bungalow next door in the early 1960s.

But happenings at our end of Jackson Road were only a small part of all that took place in Newbourne during those early days. The whole village was experiencing a time of great upheaval.

47 Jackson Road, about 1944

4 – BUILDING FOR BRITAIN

Once the Land Settlement Association had completed its purchase in Newbourne in October 1936, events moved quickly. A building contract was awarded to a local firm, Gostling and Son Ltd of Walton, Felixstowe, with quotes of £337 and £425 respectively accepted for the three-bedroomed and four-bedroomed houses. By the end of June 1937, 14 houses had been built and were occupied. Others quickly followed with all holdings on Ipswich Road and Mill Road occupied by the end of that year.

Ready for work! (John Smith)

Apart from No. 47, few holdings on Jackson Road appear to have had residents before 1939. Estate records have only Nos. 30, 32 and 33 on Jackson Road occupied in late 1937. Those living there were, respectively, W A Hedley, Greenhalgh and Stephenson. Dayson and Warren moved into Nos. 31 and 43 respectively in August 1938.

With no evidence to the contrary, we can safely assume that Jackson Road was named after Sir Percy Jackson, appointed the LSA's first chairman in 1934. At that time, Sir Percy was vice-chairman of the Carnegie Trust, one of the association's founding organisations. He was well-respected nationally as a man with a strong social conscience, as well as in his native Yorkshire where he had served since 1918 as Chairman of West Riding Education Committee. Sir Percy gave up most of his public work in 1937, but continued with the LSA until his death in 1941. The only other Jacksons linked with Newbourne seem unlikely to have been honoured in naming this narrow strip of concrete. One was Jimmy Jackson, the first occupant

24

of 10 Ipswich Road; the other was Stephen Jackson, landlord of The Fox during the 19th Century.

Potential smallholders were given three months of preparatory training, most of which was spent preparing the holdings. For some it included helping to build the houses into which they and their families would eventually move. This was followed by a further three months of more intensive training, and then an assessment. If successful, they were allocated a smallholding, and then joined by their wives and children. Throughout the first year or so, a number of trainees were accommodated in the community hut, which at that time was in the farm yard behind Newbourne Hall.

For a further twelve months, and sometimes longer, the men continued to be classed as trainees, and could continue to draw unemployment benefit and the training supplement. They just paid rent for their accommodation. Buildings and equipment on their holdings, and any marketable produce, remained the property of the LSA. Once they became tenants, they were entirely dependent on profits from their holding. Rates also became payable. Many took advantage of loans available through the LSA, repayable over 10 years.

Rents were generally between £30 and £40 per annum depending on size of house, size of holding, and number and type of other buildings. The water tower on No. 5 holding and the pump house on No. 6 each attracted a discount of 10s per annum. Holdings were

The water tower at No. 5 Ipswich Road, bordering No. 3 (The Field)

uniformly assessed for rates. Ground rent on the smaller houses was £12, the rateable value £7. For the larger houses, the ground rent was £14, the rateable value £8.

No 49 in Fenn Lane was earmarked for *"the man in charge of the water-works"*. Someone employed as a lorry

25

driver for the LSA was granted an occupancy there in October 1938, but was given a week's notice to quit in January 1940 for *"unsatisfactory driving of lorry"*! He had house and land only – a total of just over 2.5 acres – which he was required to keep in good order for £22.0s.0d pa.

Inevitably, some trainees became disillusioned, preferring their former haunts in the north-east to the relative isolation of Newbourne. Some just found the work too hard. Interestingly, I found an article in, of all places, an Australian newspaper, the *Cairns Post* of July 5th 1938, that blamed their wives:

"Attempts to turn English unemployed town-dwellers into farmers are not always successful. Thirty per cent of the unemployed men whom the Land Settlement Association has placed on the land in the past four years have gone back to their slum homes again – and their wives are to blame.

"This is what they said at the association's annual meeting in London this week. Women from the towns and cities are not as adaptable to life in the country as their menfolk. They are lonely. They miss the shops, the bright lights, the gossip.

"Sir Percy Jackson, chairman of the association, explained why more than 200 men have quitted the countryside after their training had begun.

'The average age of the men who come to us is 40; they have been out of work for four or five years, are in poor physical condition, their character weakened by long idleness.

'When they first come they cannot do a full day's work without excessive fatigue. They are suspicious and anxious. Many are inclined to give up on the most trivial excuse. One went home because his free outfit of clothes, promised by first post one morning, did not arrive till later. Another left because there was no fire in his hostel bedroom.

'When men have remained for the whole of the testing period of three months they are often unsettled by the arrival of their wives. The transfer to new conditions often proves too much for the wife. The shops are too far away; she feels isolated. Even when she, too, has remained for several months, there is no certainty that she is ready to settle.'

'But,' said Sir Percy, 'there is a bright side. Men and women who survive the training period are stronger in body, saner in mind, more self-confident, more hopeful, and the change in their children is even more marked. They have shaken off their dependence on the dole, and

are ready to make an independent career for themselves.'"

To me, Sir Percy's remarks, presumably endorsed by the rest of the LSA's top brass, betray a somewhat paternalistic approach. This may not have been out of place in the first half of the 20th Century. It probably underpinned much of the philanthropy and humanitarian work of that era. But once the war was over, many tenants with previous agricultural and horticultural training and experience were recruited. Some of the early settlers, too, had become experienced and knowledgeable horticulturists. Yet this attitude continued to inform many decisions made centrally by both government and the LSA.

Much more on this can be found in *Appendix D – The Land Settlement Association: its rise and demise*. However, I am not alone in maintaining that it was an approach to social improvement that ultimately led to the association's closure amid much acrimony in 1983. Ironically, it was only then that these men were free to fulfil Sir Percy's vision to *"make an independent career for themselves"*.

A report to Head Office from the estate manager at that time said of the trainees: *"They are appearing to show more interest in their work and appear to be liking the living very much better than they*

View from the water tower, Ipswich Road, in 1946 (The Field)

did." He added that, *"in view of the rather poor state of the soil, the crops look considerably better than might be expected."*

At the outset, *"the rather poor state of the soil"* on some holdings was a matter of some concern. Another report from the manager to LSA Head Office included the following assessment:

Holding	Comment
10	"Very poor land at back"
12	"Back land very poor"
15	"Poor land this, and under hedge"
16	"Poorer, and has waste pit land"
17a	"Old crag pit in centre"
21	"Rough marshy holding, trees etc"
22	"In very rough state"
24	"Was rough pasture"
26	"Rough, similar to 21"
29	"Poorer land"
41	"Useful arable land at top end"
45	"10% allowance for hedge down centre of holding"

And why were holdings 40 to 43 in Jackson Road numbered out of sequence? Apparently, Nos. 40 and 42 should have been built on the opposite side of the road. But the land there was too wet, so they had to be squeezed in on land allocated to Nos. 41 and 43 respectively.

Stringing outdoor tomatoes, mid-'40s (LSA Charitable Trust)

28

According to estate records for June 1938, 28 trainees were resident on holdings and two in the hut, but no-one had yet been granted a tenancy. Estate staff would have occupied up to five of the houses. By April 1939, 13 trainees had been granted tenancies, a figure that rose to 23 by the end of January 1940, when there were also 24 trainees and 4 vacancies. It appears that some houses were later used for short periods during the war by services personnel.

At that point the LSA had 21 estates throughout England. This represented 1030 smallholdings, of which 785 were occupied either by tenants or trainees and 245 vacant.

(See *The holdings in more detail* on the next page)

THE HOLDINGS IN MORE DETAIL

It is fair to assume that the LSA was keen to have the estate operational as early as possible, and so initially concentrated on constructing houses and holdings on Ipswich Road and Mill Road where they had ready access. This is supported by local historian, Walter Tye, in the *East Anglian Magazine* in March 1961, who wrote: *"Lastly, the new Jackson Road was constructed, the early trainees doing much of the work."* I remember that one of them had scratched the year of construction in the concrete edge of the road outside No. 36, but I've forgotten what it was! The concrete was broken up long ago.

An undated LSA internal memo indicates that an early plan was to develop the ten *"greenhouse holdings"* first. These were Nos. 18, 19, 20, 21, 22, 24, 26, 27, 28 and 48. All were in Mill Road except 48, which was opposite the chapel. No. 49 – in Fenn Lane and earmarked for *"the man in charge of the waterworks"* – was also to be built at this stage.

Next would be the twelve *"poultry holdings"*. These were Nos. 5, 7, 9, 10, 11, 12, 13, 14, 15 and 16 on Ipswich Road plus 31 and 35 on Jackson Road. Last of all were the *"watercress holdings"* – Nos. 30, 32, 33, 34, 36, 38, 39, 40, 42, 44, 46, all on Jackson Road plus 50, 51 and 52 on Woodbridge Road.

The memo made no mention of Nos. 1, 2, 3, 4, 6 and 8 on Ipswich Road, so it must have been written after they were completed. They were certainly all occupied by October 1937. A photo in the book, *Village life in and around Felixstowe* by John Smith, Neil Wylie, Peter White and Phil Hadwen, shows *"the first settlers . . . . outside the rectory, after the first house, No. 1 Ipswich Road, was completed for them in 1936-37."* The photo is reproduced in the next chapter with the authors' kind permission. Also omitted from the memo but completed by October 1937 were 17, 17a, 23, 25, 25a and 29 on Mill Road. No. 23a on Mill Road – probably a staff house – was either not built or at least unoccupied at that time.

Dates for No. 37, 41, 43, 45 and 47 are unclear, but will have been first occupied during 1938 or 1939.

5 – HERE COME THE GEORDIES (AND OTHERS)

Mention Newbourne and the Land Settlement Association, and many will respond, *"Oh, isn't that where the miners used to live?"*

It is true that most of the very early settlers were drawn from the ranks of the unemployed in the industrial north-east. One or two are reputed to have come from south Wales. But some had never been miners – just long-term unemployed. It needs to be remembered, too, that, once the war had started and the LSA had begun recruiting men with agricultural experience – so-called Agricultural Tenants – other dialects began to compete with Geordie in The Fox.

Among the original settlers was Ivy Griffiths' family, the Cheshers, from Horden in County Durham. Ivy moved away from Newbourne in the early 1940s to train as a nurse but after her husband died in the mid-1990s, she returned to the village to care for her brother. She has lived there ever since and has a fund of stories of those early days.

Her parents, Alf and Alice Maud, arrived in Newbourne in October 1937, together with Ivy, her younger sister Jean and older brother Alfie. Alf had just completed six months as one of a group of eight trainees, and had been granted the tenancy of No. 17a on Mill Road.

A smallholding in Newbourne had seemed like a good idea to Alf. He had been a POW in WW1 and had had little success in finding work after leaving the army. After training, he reported to Alice that Newbourne was *"a bit bleak"*, but they agreed to give it a go. Their son, Alfie, was in poor health, and

Alf Chesher tending chrysanthemums, about 1961 (East Anglian Magazine)

31

Above: Mill Road in the 1930s, looking north from outside No. 17a.
Newbourne Hall is in the centre background. (John Somerville)

Alice felt that some fresh air would be good for him. Her faith in Newbourne fresh air was clearly justified – Alfie worked for many years on the holding, and died in 2003, aged 84.

The family travelled down by train, and enjoyed tea provided by the LSA in the community hut on their arrival. Ivy recalls oak trees forming an arch over Mill Road near their new house, scraping the roofs of passing buses. Their front door was accessed along a pathway through brambles.

She also remembers that the houses were very cold. On their arrival, her father poked his head into the loft of their new home and could see the sky between the roof tiles! It is unclear who was responsible for omitting to line the roofs with felt, but the failure was soon rectified.

In summer 1939, the Madgwick family arrived. George had completed his six-month training period with the LSA, and moved into No. 19 Mill Road with his wife Hannah and children, Mary, Georgie and Audrey. George had spent many years on the dole in Sunderland, supporting his family on 15 shillings a week dole money, which Georgie recalls he always collected wearing his best suit. In common with many others, he supplemented this meagre sum by selling coal found on the beach in Sunderland, which had not many

32

years before prospered as the largest shipbuilding town in Britain.

The move to Newbourne for the family was a bit of a money-making exercise in itself. The LSA covered the costs of each family's removal van. *"No-one had much furniture,"* Georgie remembers, *"so we and the Coates family from Ipswich Road shared a van, but charged for one each."*

George Madgwick and Bobby Bradley outside the Fox (Georgie Madgwick)

Many holdings were allocated simply by drawing numbers from a hat. George had drawn No. 38, but agreed to swap with Joe Webb, already living at No. 19, who wanted to be nearer a friend in Jackson Road. No. 19 was opposite the Cheshers. *"Alf used to call every morning,"* said Georgie, *"including Christmas Day."* He would always sit in their kitchen on a Geordie cracket stool – a low stool with a hole in the seat by which it could be picked up. Georgie remembers there were often arguments when Alf was around. This was especially so at tenants' meetings attended by representatives from LSA Head Office.

Arthur Locke, ca 1961 (East Anglian Magazine)

One of the first Agricultural Tenants was Arthur Locke. With his wife, May, and children Nelson and Rosalind, Arthur had the first tenancy of No. 35 Jackson Road from 1939. He had previously been a farm manager at Witnesham and also a blacksmith, and had originally wanted his own farm. With first aid and hairdressing skills, he contributed much to the community. He was also in charge of the chapel during the war, offering hospitality to visiting preachers and supporting overseas missionaries with the proceeds of his hairdressing.

Mary Sharland, who now lives in Ipswich, was the youngest of four sisters and two brothers, the children of Richard "Dick" Gratton and his wife Georgina (aka Alice). They were the first tenants of No. 16 Ipswich Road, where they lived from 1936 until 1941 or 1942. The Grattons were from the north-east, where Richard had been a miner. Mary, aged nine in 1936, still remembers the Lamb family next door at No. 14 and the Proudfoots opposite at No. 15.

Other early arrivals included Richard and Eva Vickerstaff, and their children Doreen, Marion, Edith, Richard and Olga. They were from Spennymoor, Co Durham, and in 1937 became the first to live at No. 11 Ipswich Road. It seems that Eva was a remarkable woman. According to Richard Jr, she was born in the workhouse, and spent much of her childhood there. She was self-educated, and in Newbourne was a staunch Labour supporter. She helped in the chapel Sunday School and was known for her good works. Eva died in 1947, and Richard Sr moved to Bristol soon afterwards.

Jim and Sadie Sample came from the north-east with their son, Laurie and daughter, Joyce. In September 1939 they moved into No. 52 Woodbridge Road, at

Jim Sample, about 1961 (East Anglian Magazine)

the top of what we as a family always referred to as Samples' Hill. Laurie later continued the family tradition with his own smallholding at No. 9 Ipswich Road, where he still lives. The names of most of the other early settlers are in Appendix A.

Some of the first settlers outside the rectory following completion of the first house, No. 1 Ipswich Road: L to R: Back row – Adam Smith, W Hedley, Turner, Alf Hedley, unknown, Jack Wilder, F Proudfoot, J Raine. Middle row – Dick Gratton, Fred Jarrett, Jimmy Jackson, unknown, C Roberts, Longworth. Front row – unknown, G Iceton, Dick Vickerstaff, J Johnston, J Narey, unknown, unknown. (John Smith)

The incoming Geordies found the Suffolk dialect difficult to understand, while the native Suffolk-speakers must have felt they had been invaded by an alien race. Hostilities occasionally erupted, especially in the early days. The newcomers were certainly not immediately welcomed by the Fox's regular customers.

Two other obstacles to harmonious community relations tend to be overlooked. One, as Richard Vickerstaff pointed out, was that the Geordies, although all from the north-east, did not always understand one another's dialect, let alone that of the locals! The other, he explained, was that, while many were more than happy to patronise The Fox, to the strict Methodists among them, *"it was nothing less than the gates of hell"*.

6 - NEWBOURNE HALL AND THE FARM

The LSA paid George Denn Turner £7,250 for the 471 acres. This included £2,400 for buildings including Newbourne Hall, several cottages and Lower House Farm. The purchase did not include Street Farm on Hemley Road or Walk Barn Farm on Woodbridge Road, which had both been sold long before. Selling the hall and the estate will not have been easy during the agricultural depression of the 1930s. Some years previously it had been unsuccessfully marketed for £12,500.

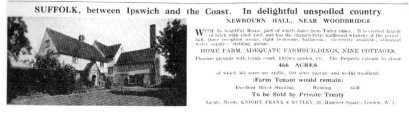

SUFFOLK, between Ipswich and the Coast. In delightful unspoiled country
NEWBOURN HALL, NEAR WOODBRIDGE

WITH its beautiful House, part of which dates from Tudor times. It is erected largely of brick with tiled roof, and has the characteristic mullioned windows of the period; hall, three reception rooms, eight bedrooms, bathroom; electricity available; abundant water supply; stabling, garage.

HOME FARM, ADEQUATE FARMBUILDINGS, NINE COTTAGES.

Pleasure grounds with tennis court, kitchen garden, etc. The Property extends to about

466 ACRES

of which 365 acres are arable, 100 acres pasture and useful woodland.

(Farm Tenant would remain)

Excellent Mixed Shooting.   Hunting.   Golf.

To be Sold by Private Treaty

Agents, Messrs. KNIGHT, FRANK & RUTLEY, 20, Hanover Square, London, W. 1.

From Country Life, 21ˢᵗ September 1935 (from John Somerville)

After the sale, George Turner, aged 80 and with a reputation as a tough businessman and a firm disciplinarian, moved to Felixstowe with his daughter Dorothy and son Charles, where they lived in White Lodge in Ferry Road. Dorothy returned to Newbourne in 1954, and lived in Brook Cottage on the corner of The Street and Woodbridge Road until a few years before her death. Leslie and Norah Dow had been tenants at Brook Cottage from 1936. Leslie had been a tea planter in South Africa. In 1952 they bought the old rectory on Ipswich Road, moving there the following year.

A year or so after their purchase, the Land Settlement Association sold off what is now the 40-acre Newbourne Springs Nature Reserve to the Felixstowe Water Company for £620. This was known then as Alder Carr or Newbourne Carr, and by local children as the Primrose Woods. A Miss Tilley bought the cottage in which she then lived for £10. This was the last property on the right in Fenn Lane, which was commonly known as Pit Lane according to the deeds of purchase of the estate. Also, compensation was paid to C C Smith and Sons, who had had to relinquish the tenancy of Hall Farm.

There seems to have been some early difficulty in obtaining

sufficient mains water pressure for holdings on Ipswich Road. A water tower was constructed on No. 5's land on its border with No. 3. This was kept filled by the now derelict pumping station at the end of Fenn Lane, which also fed the three holdings – 50, 51 and 52 – on Woodbridge Road. Leslie and Nora Dow's son David remembered helping Herbert Frost supply water for mixing the concrete used in building those three houses. Herbert used a horse-drawn bowser, which he filled from Newbourne Stream near Brook Cottage. David, aged about 10, was allowed to lead the Suffolk Punches up the hill and then ride them on the way back. Herbert's grandson, Michael, with a family connection to the two Newbourne Giants – brothers George Page (7ft 7in) and Meadows Page (7ft 5in) – now owns Highfield Farm at the top of the same hill.

The former yard and buildings of Hall Farm behind Newbourne Hall became the LSA's local headquarters, with office, packing shed, and stores. Initially, an old barn on the southern edge of the farm was used as the packing shed. This is evident from the photo, published in *The Field* in June 1947, showing produce being unloaded there from a horse-drawn cart. This building was later used as the estate's stores. A larger purpose-built packing shed was erected in 1953 immediately behind the hall. 76 acres of land

The first packing shed, later the stores
(The Field)

on the higher ground behind the farm was cultivated for some years by the Estate Service Department as a "fruit block", used, at least initially, for blackcurrants.

Propagation of plants was an essential part of the support provided for tenants on all LSA estates. In Newbourne this was initially carried out behind No. 48 opposite the chapel, but it was later moved to the land behind the farm. The "prop" was also used to demonstrate best growing practice.

The "prop" behind No. 48, with church and chapel in the background, 1946.
(The Field)

Georgie Madgwick remembers the community hut erected by the LSA where the new packing shed was later built. This had a stage and was used for village social activities before the war and, I think, for accommodating some of the early trainees. When war broke out, older children from the village were no longer allowed to cross Martlesham aerodrome to school at Kesgrave, and had to be taught at Waldringfield. Evacuee children were taught in the old Waldringfield village hall next door. Younger children had to stay in Newbourne to free up space at Waldringfield, and were educated in the hut, with a Mrs Cooper as their first teacher.

The hut's use as a school was later regularised. Estate records note that *"the hut situate in the farmyard adjoining Newbourne Hall* [is] *made available to East Suffolk C C for use as a Public Elementary School on 1st December 1940."* The Local Education Authority was *"answerable to the Association for any injury done to any sheep cattle pigs or other animals upon the land belonging to the Association."* No-one seemed to be answerable for any injury to the children. The rent was £13.0s.0d per annum, with rates and taxes paid by the LSA.

The estate's warden or manager in February 1938 was Bernard Davey, although the first warden may have been Ernest Brown, who

38

lived in the Hall during 1937. Bernard Davey was succeeded by David Angus in mid-1938. At some point the estate manager, and his wife who apparently hated living in the Hall, moved into No. 48 opposite the chapel. *"The LSA were going to bulldoze the Hall,"* says Ivy Griffiths, *"but then let the doctor have a surgery there. It was very run down, with a leaky roof and buckets to catch the drips. It was also used two nights each week for a youth club."*

Ivy also mentioned that her father donated a billiard table to the Hall. This had initially been used in their living room at 17a, but was really too big. I certainly remember seeing the table when we collected our government-issue orange juice and cod liver oil from Newbourne Hall before Mrs Cornell took responsibility for supplying them from Street Farm. John Somerville, owner of the Hall since 1977, says that some of the dents made by billiard cues still remain in the 17th century plaster ceiling of what is now his drawing room. He and his father before him decided to leave them as historical evidence.

As time passed, the Hall became an important centre of community life. Both John Hedley and I recall a maypole on the front lawn, and Georgie Madgwick remembers a woodwork room where Joe Coates used to take woodwork classes. There was also a cricket pitch behind the estate office. *"My father persuaded the man operating the road roller to roll the cricket square,"* he said, adding that his father was also responsible for sports, and that his mother held dancing lessons. Mary Sharland recalls children's dancing and being taken in an army lorry to entertain the troops stationed in Kirton.

Newbourne Hall, about 1900 (John Somerville)

It seems that Newbourne Hall was always something of a bugbear to the LSA. This listed Tudor and early Stuart manor house, with parts dating back to the 14th Century, was once owned by Cardinal Thomas Wolsey and associated with Queen Catherine Parr. But this seems to have meant little to the association, particularly in the early days of the war. Having only reluctantly decided against bulldozing it, in 1942 they advertised for a tenant, with the rent set at £60 per annum. No tenants materialised, and the Hall continued to be used as a social centre. Later it was used by the army until the end of the war, by which time it was in a very sorry state. It was then rented by Stuart Somerville, who moved there with his family in 1945.

One or two in the LSA hierarchy did appreciate the hall's historic and architectural features, and were pleased to have tenants who felt the same. Stuart was the son of artist and collector Charles Somerville.

According to the website, www.suffolkpainters.co.uk, Stuart was a painter of landscapes, flowers, figures and interiors. He exhibited at the Royal Academy in 1925 aged 17, the youngest to do so since Landseer, and continued to do so until 1961. He was a member of Ipswich Art Club, and painted until his death in 1983. Stuart's sister Margaret, always known as Peggy, was a child prodigy who learned to paint at the same time she learned to walk. She became a land girl in 1942, moving with her widowed mother to join Stuart and Catherine in Newbourne Hall in 1945.

Once the LSA had erected its new packing shed close to the west side of the property, plans were made to site a village hall in the hall's garden to the north. Then they decided to use the hall's gardens on the opposite side of the road as the site for a new house for the estate manager. A suggestion that the hall be demolished to allow more direct access to the packing shed, office and stores was the last straw. Stuart and Catherine Somerville pressed hard for the LSA to sell them the hall and its immediate garden, and were eventually able to agree a sale on 22nd May 1957. A programme of restoration and refurbishment has continued to this day.

7 – NOSES TO THE GRINDSTONE

How I wish I had spent time with my parents before they died, getting them to fill the gaps between my sometimes sketchy memories of our early years at No. 47. In my late teens and early twenties, there were times when my father and I sat down together. But, sadly, they were all too often wasted in pointless arguments about politics or religion. Now it's too late.

There is much that I should have asked. As I discovered in the LSA's 1939 review, No. 47 had been described as an *"odd sort of holding, obviously unsuited to intensive horticultural development"*. So how did it become the productive and economically viable unit that was sold in 1967 when my father died? What were the highs and lows, the successes and failures? How hard was it for them to provide food, clothing and a good education for three demanding, energetic boys?

What I do know is that, during the war, when Britain was almost entirely dependent on what it could grow itself, there was a ready market for more or less anything edible. To start with, we grew tomatoes and lettuce in the greenhouse as well as outdoors, with the lettuce starting life under cloches or cold frames. At various times we grew beetroot, radishes, artichokes, asparagus, peas, black and red currants, gooseberries, strawberries, raspberries, turnips, potatoes, cultivated blackberries, and even 3 to 4 acres of barley. LSA records include an order for sugar beet seed in December 1942, but I have no memory of it ever being used. Free-range chickens enabled us to sell birds for slaughter as well as eggs, while pigs came and went on a regular basis. We also kept a goat.

Alf Chesher once remarked that he never thought he would say that Hitler was his best friend. *"But the war meant we could sell anything in any quantity,"* said Ivy. And, of course, there was usually enough for the smallholders' own families, too. *"We were never really short of food during the war,"* she said, *"even though money was often short."*

With apples and plums from the old Lower House orchard, blackberries in Sandy Lane, bullace plums on the Bucklesham side of the valley, and watercress from the little stream, our recommended *"5 portions-a-day"* diet of fruit and veg was assured. Mr Pask, the butcher, delivered regularly from Felixstowe in his van, but the pheasants, partridges and rabbits shot with my father's 12-bore must have ensured that rationing was not as much an imposition as it was for many. Close encounters with bones, feathers, and assorted intestines became part of our lives. And I'll never forget the large, cured portion of one of our pigs that confronted anyone opening the cupboard under the stairs. Strangely, I don't remember eating chicken, although we may have consumed the unfortunate hen that refused to leave the long grass between us and No. 46. After its head was neatly removed by the hay cutter, it flew around for some time like a – well, headless chicken.

Some smallholders at least were aware of others less fortunate (that's people, not chickens). During the war, Alf Chesher once found a family messing about on the roadside adjacent to his holding.

"Is this your land, mister?

"Yes," said Alf. *"What are you doing?"*

"We're from Ipswich, and we're getting nettles to make into soup," came the unexpected reply.

Alf had never heard of nettle soup, but he asked them to stop. Telling them to wait, he went back to the house, and returned with three bags and a spade. Pointing up the holding, he said,

"Go up to that field. You'll find plenty of carrots and turnips. You can take as many as you need," adding, *"but you're not to sell them."*

"You'll never want for nothing, mister," they shouted over their shoulders, as they ran up the holding.

Alf had asked for the bags to be returned, but they never were.

Ivy remembers much neighbourliness during early days on the estate.

The Cheshers' house and holding in the background, seen from No. 23 (Sue Whittaker)

42

"Everyone was so helpful and friendly – not like now," she says. Dick Whittaker's smallholding was No. 23, next door to the Cheshers and opposite the Madgwicks. In his unpublished book about Newbourne, Dick remarked on the friendliness of his Geordie neighbours.

Early in the war, with rationing well under way, my parents posted a dozen and a half eggs to friends in Kent. Only two arrived cracked. *"They are so large and such a lovely flavour,"* wrote the grateful recipients. But not all were as appreciative. An aunt from Romford came to stay during the war or soon after, and complained that her boiled egg at breakfast was old and had *"gone off"*. In fact, it had been taken from the nest that morning.

Some who lived locally took longer than others to adapt to country ways. Georgie Madgwick remembers the local policeman, PC Burgoyne from Kirton, speaking once to the Young Farmer's Club. He told about a woman he knew, who complained that her new chicks were not doing at all well.

"What do you feed the on?", asked the officer.

"I don't feed them on anything." she said. *"I thought the mother fed them."*

An abiding memory for us boys is the smell emanating from the large boiler in the piggery. This was used for boiling potatoes as well as the regular deliveries of swill from Footman's restaurant in Ipswich. What Footman's customers rejected, the pigs enjoyed immensely, snorting and squealing impatiently as

it was tipped into their troughs. The odd pieces of elegant cutlery that graced our dining table were a bonus, although I think that less upmarket swill was also available from the RAF, presumably at Martlesham aerodrome.

Tenants learned to take set-backs in their stride. I clearly remember the large pit dug in the craggy soil immediately behind the piggery, and the carcase of a diseased adult pig being buried. My father's glum expression will have reflected a concern at our own financial loss rather than any sadness for the pig.

Another pit was dug a few years later when a glut of tomatoes meant it was cheaper to bury them than send them to market. On one occasion, an eel-worm infestation meant that a complete greenhouse of lettuce had to be destroyed. Michael recalls that one winter was so mild that there was a glut of large lettuces: *"We had to strip the outer leaves off the 18s to make them fit 24 to a crate to reduce transportation costs,"* he said.

Coping with the stress of these mishaps must have been hard, but our parents generally succeeded in keeping their feelings to themselves. And there were good times, too: one morning ours were the only lettuces in Covent Garden!

Ready for market (Nick Packer)

As time passed, smallholders, with an eye to the market, tended to concentrate on crops giving the best return. They recognised the benefits of specialising in either produce or stock, and the importance of the economy of scale. My father, from trying to grow or rear almost anything that could be eaten, moved to specialising in tomatoes, lettuces and poultry.

Our battery house began to fulfil its primary function. Rows of battery cages were purchased, supplies of feed and water laid on, and chickens installed. Eggs duly began rolling down the sloping floors on which each bird spent its life, and came to rest, pristine, to await collection. Droppings were collected in trays below. I don't remember anyone questioning the battery system that many people nowadays regard as inhumane.

The benefits of growing tomatoes and lettuces under glass were soon recognised, especially in the face of competition from Dutch growers. In addition to their relatively small, standard greenhouses,

44

many tenants invested in the larger Dutchlight structures, adding to them as the years passed. Seedlings were propagated centrally at *"the Prop"* or by growers themselves under cold frames or cloches. Laurie Sample remembers my father as the first to use under-soil heating, This was powered through a large transformer, which he also used to thaw underground water pipes during the hard winter of 1963. At some stage, Arthur Gilder used the transformer for the same purpose elsewhere in the village, towing it on a trailer behind his car.

My father, together with Wally Hammond at 22 Mill Road and John Wild at 32 Jackson Road, worked on a number of initiatives to increase tomato production. One of these was *"trickle irrigation"*, which used narrow-gauge rubber hoses laid along each row. Water pressure was adjusted to deliver very small amounts of water through a nozzle alongside each plant. Jeremy remembers our father also working with a smallholder in Nacton or Levington on cordoning tomato plants. Instead of pinching out the tops of the plants, they trained them horizontally, using the strings of adjacent plants. The result was up to 18 trusses per plant instead of the usual half dozen.

Produce from all the holdings was sorted and packed for market in the packing shed behind Newbourne Hall. Ted Baxter and Jack Wicks were among those responsible for taking the produce several times a week to wholesale markets in London, Birmingham and Manchester. The London lorries needed to leave at between 7pm and 8pm, with Covent Garden opening at midnight, Spitalfields at 5am and Stratford at 6am. The busy period, says Ted, was between March and November.

Ted recalls that increasing competition from the Canary Islands and elsewhere in the late 1950s meant that LSA produce *"took a hammering"*. At one stage, Birds Eye at Lowestoft and Yarmouth were given the pick of the crop before what they rejected was repacked and taken to London and elsewhere. Some tenants' produce from Newbourne was regarded as substandard, and buyers in the markets put pressure on the lorry drivers to be given first choice. Ted was uncomfortable with this and asked to be relieved of the market run. He eventually left the LSA in 1959.

Right from the beginning, there were threats from bugs and diseases. With more intensive production under glass, these threats increased. I always remember stern warnings to keep clear of the glasshouses when greenfly were being dealt with. This involved

45

burning small heaps of sulphur placed at intervals along the paths between rows of tomato plants. Early on, soil sterilisation was carried out using the estate's steam-driven traction engine. Flexible copper pipes, with small holes along their length, were buried at what I think was a spade's-depth, and steam forced through them for a set period. The piping would then be moved and re-buried, and the process repeated. It was a time-consuming and back-breaking job.

Moles were dispatched using our own mole traps. According to Jeanne Gilder's son Barry, they were sometimes dealt with by Bill Pettitt using *"strychnine-impregnated worms."* Bill Mather from Waldringfield was responsible for hedges and ditches, and clearing what in Suffolk are called *"watergrups"* – channels cut in the verges to allow water to flow from the roads into the ditches. He also laid hedges using the traditional method of cutting part-way through the growing wooden stems and weaving them together horizontally. Bill's hedges were works of art, appreciated by people and wildlife alike.

Weasels and stoats, a particular threat to young game birds, were frequently shot and their bodies hung from fences, presumably to deter their fellows. Ivy Griffiths remembers boys using sticks to catch rats. They would present the tails, in bundles wrapped in paper with just the tips showing, at the Estate Office, where they would earn a

Stoat: "a threat" (en.wikipedia.org)

penny per tail. Ivy once caught three, cut the tails in half before bundling them, and was paid sixpence. When her father learned how much she'd been paid, he said, *"But you only caught three rats."* When Ivy confessed, her father's friend standing nearby commented: *"She'll go places!"*

"The only place she's going is bed," said her father. Ivy recalls with gratitude that her parents *"were known in the family for always commending honesty and truth."*

A variant on cutting tails in half was practised by John Hedley and his mates. He remembers being given only a halfpenny per rat's tail, but confesses to making up the difference by breaking in around the back of the office at night to *"nick a few tails and sell them back the next day."*

The east coast floods of 1953, described in a later chapter, dealt a huge blow to tenants of low-lying land in Mill Road and Jackson Road. Alf Chesher was not one of them, but Ivy remembers her family and others having to take precautions against another threat at about the same time. Outbreaks of foot and mouth disease had been reported in several counties, with many pigs slaughtered. *"We had a tank of disinfectant for our feet outside our back door,"* she says.

So much of what we did was affected by the weather. Weather forecasts in those days were notoriously unreliable for periods of longer than 24 hours or so, and yet a smallholder's income potential could be severely compromised if he failed to prepare for unexpected changes. In any case, my father always reckoned that Newbourne's weather was rarely as forecast anyway, since it was largely determined by the two rivers, the Orwell and Deben between which Newbourne was sandwiched. Informed decision-making was essential if produce was not to reach the market in the middle of a glut.

Arthur and Jeanne Gilder arrived in Newbourne in May 1946, and lived for the first two-and-a-half years at No. 4 on the Ipswich Road. Arthur had recently left the Royal Navy, where he had been a Petty Officer in radar. He had earlier served an apprenticeship as a carpenter, and came to the village as estate handyman. Arthur was a real Jack-of-all-trades, but not even he could have imagined how his practical skills would be used during the following winter. From mid-January to mid-March 1947, some of the lowest temperatures on record caused great hardship across the country. Arthur's job each night throughout that long winter was to climb the estate's water tower at No. 5 and hang a lighted brazier close to the pipes to stop them freezing. Arthur could put his hand to anything. What the estate would have done without him, I cannot imagine.

The deep snow was slow to melt, and Jeanne remembers Mrs Swann wearing snow shoes when delivering the post. Coal was in short supply, and power was rationed. *"After that, I vowed I'd never spend another winter in Newbourne,"* said Jeanne. *"I've never been so cold."* But stay she did, and in November 1948 moved to No. 42 on Jackson Road. She and Arthur, with their first two children, Lindy and Barry, moved into No. 44 next door in the early '50s. Their youngest son, Keith, was born soon afterwards. Jeanne spent many years working with my father, and is still at No. 44, shortly to celebrate her 90th birthday.

Jeanne Gilder painting our greenhouse (J Gilder)

8 - LIVING ABOVE THE SHOP

Separating family life from working life was never straightforward for tenants on any of the LSA's estates. Living above the shop is always a challenge, but especially so when both home and shop are owned by someone else.

For tenants during the late thirties, the challenge was made harder by the initial six months of training spent away from family and friends. It is possible that a few wives had become accustomed to having an unemployed husband under their feet for much of the day, and will have welcomed the change. But many will have found it hard to cope. And children will have missed their fathers, particularly those too young to appreciate the reasons. Even after their families had joined them, many men in Newbourne had to work long hours outside making the generally poor land fit for cultivation.

Once a tenant had established home and holding, and begun to see some financial reward for his efforts, his family would usually be expected to provide additional labour on an on-going basis. Without the white goods and other labour-saving devices we are used to, women in Newbourne already had much to keep them occupied in the home. But now feeding the family had to compete for time with feeding the chickens and pigs. Hands that were red and raw from washing up and washing clothes were sometimes dark green from picking tomatoes or removing sideshoots.

Families provided additional labour
(LSA Charitable Trust)

Children were inevitably drawn into the operation. The very young observed these activities from a safe distance. Some were in prams or pushchairs, but one or two were probably in lettuce crates or even wheelbarrows. Older children would find much lying around with which to amuse themselves – from hand tools to large balls of string, from buckets to hosepipes. Lettuce crates could be stacked as fortifications, while rotten tomatoes were the obvious choice of ammunition.

Danger was never far away. Each holding had a greenhouse, but it was the glass *"structures"* that needed the greatest care. Their walls and roofs were constructed entirely from Dutchlights – 5ft by 2ft 6in glass panes in a wooden frame. In hot weather, some were temporarily removed to provide ventilation. Most glass was frosted, but not all. In later years, while working in our oldest structure, I heard my father

My father in one of our Dutchlight structures

call me from outside. Sprinting along the path between two rows of plants, I headed for a gap where a Dutchlight had been removed – or so I thought! Landing at my horrified father's feet in a shower of broken glass, I suffered only a very small cut on my forehead.

All this changed, especially as we approached our teens. Ros Hart's father, Arthur Locke, had the tenancy of No. 35 on Jackson Road. Ros remembers there being little time for play. *"We were expected to help on the holding,"* she says. Ros trained as a secretary, and after a period with Ransome Sims & Jefferies in Ipswich, was taken on by the LSA to work in the Newbourne estate office. Here strict confidentiality was vital as her father was chairman of the estate tenants' association.

For some young people, an alternative to working on the holding was helping in the home to free up their mothers for work outside. Ivy Griffiths sometimes cooked for the family to help her mother, but left home aged 17. She came home occasionally but had to avoid tomato plants because the green hands that resulted were not appreciated by the hospital sister where she was training as a nurse!

Ivy recalls that a sudden demand for leeks once led to the entire Chesher family – her parents, herself and her brother and sister – pulling leeks from dawn to dusk. The whole lot – a lorry load – went to Covent Garden that night. No-one minded the backache until Alf later calculated that, taking marketing costs into account, he had ended up owing the estate 1s 6d!

The three of us at No. 47 often endured a 5.30am start to our school day. Lettuces had to be cut and stacked in crates at the roadside ready for collection by the estate's lorry or tractor. This had to be done early enough to avoid produce deteriorating in the midday sun. With our holding being farthest from the central packing shed, any protest from us that our school mates would have nearly two hours longer in bed fell on deaf ears. We did our best to ignore fingers numbed by cold and wet lettuce, and focussed our thoughts on the pocket money that would accrue. Michael clearly recalls doing an hour and a half's lettuce packing on Tuesdays before school, and at the other end of the day arriving home from Ipswich at 5.15pm for tea and homework before cycling to his violin lesson at 7.00pm with Mr Sutton at Waldringfield. After cycling home, there was often more homework before bed.

Living at the far end of Jackson Road must have made it hard for my parents to develop any form of social life. It would have been especially difficult for the first few years with no car or telephone. Apart from the postman, butcher, coal man and baker, the only adults I saw on a daily basis were connected with my father's work. Wally Ball or his brother, Billy, or Bill and Fred Pettitt would arrive most days by tractor and trailer or lorry to collect the tomatoes, lettuces or eggs we had left at the side of the road. Billy Ball and his sister Winnie lived in Red House just past Street Farm on the road to Hemley.

On our arrival in 1942, our neighbours at No. 46 were the Friends. When the war ended, they were followed by Ernie and Florrie Wicks from Hemley. At No. 45 were Fred and Ethel Pettitt, with son Bill. They were followed by Mr and Mrs Ruffle, with daughters Ann and Mary. However, the family we had most contact with lived at No. 40. Harry and Molly Cracknell became life-long friends of my parents. Their children, Diana and Christopher, were our earliest playmates.

"Earliest playmates": From left – Diana and Christopher Cracknell, Michael, unknown, author

For the first few years, our nearest telephone was half a mile away at the village end of Jackson Road. We learned how to press Button A when the call was answered and Button B to get our money back if it wasn't. In 1946, telephone poles were erected the length of Jackson Road so that we could have our own phone – well, not exactly our own, as it was a party line shared with John and Katie Wild at No 32. This was not ideal as we could each hear the other's conversations, as well as interference from the pirate radio stations!

Occasionally there would be deliveries of anthracite for the glasshouse boilers or sacks of fertiliser and meal. Sometimes the estate manager or another official would drop in on business. Pigs arrived and departed in lorries with much grunting and squealing, and day-old chicks were delivered from Ipswich station. With much ooh-ing and aah-ing, we loved watching them scamper about under the infra-red lamps as they were tipped unceremoniously from octagonal cardboard boxes into their new quarters.

All in all it was hard to switch off at the end of the day. My father, only an occasional drinker, was never one for spending his leisure time or money in the Fox. The round trip of nearly three miles on foot or bike made it even less attractive. When ventilators had been closed, boilers stoked and returns for the day's produce completed, helping us with maths homework was probably needed before he could fill his pipe at last and occupy his favourite armchair. More than once, after a particularly hard week, he would pick up the paper or the *Farmer and Stockbreeder* on Sunday evening, light his pipe and announce: *"Let the weekend begin!"*.

Socials and concerts in the Village Hall were irregular highlights in a very restricted social calendar. Our mother, who could often be heard singing songs from the '20s and '30s around the house – and, if the windows were open, around the holding – had a reasonable voice. It was probably wasted on the rest of her family, but her renditions of *Charmaine* and *Over the rainbow* earned considerable applause in Newbourne Village Hall. Performing to an audience was not my father's cup of tea, although he was always ready to help behind the scenes. In the company of other smallholders, it was all too easy to spend the evening talking shop. Animated discussion concerned esoteric subjects like botritis, didymella, cladosporium and eel worm. Sometimes it was just about LSA head office.

Others who were part of our lives included casual workers assisting during the busier times. One of the earliest came during our first spring in Newbourne. Ivy was a landgirl, described by my mother as *"hopeless – she'd been a cinema usherette!"*. She had her bed on straw bales in the battery house, no doubt grateful that our chickens were free range at the time. Two local teenagers, together with Ivy, helped out during early 1943 when my father was in bed for a month with a duodenal ulcer, I had measles and Michael needed weaning on to solid food.

We were also allocated a German prisoner-of-war, but still needed to use local labour from time to time. Georgie Madgwick remembers being my father's fastest blackcurrant picker, probably in the late 1940s. Come payday, he would always hand his earnings to his mother. On one occasion, his grandparents, visiting from Tyneside, were horrified to see what Georgie had earned. *"It was more than my grandfather earned in the pit!,"* said Georgie.

Jeanne Gilder was really my father's right-hand woman throughout much of the 1950s and 1960s. Mrs G (Mrs Gilder, of course, to us children) worked for several tenants in Newbourne over the years, but as the work at No. 47 grew, she became effectively full-time on our holding. She took on increasing responsibility, and always appreciated my father's willingness to give her instructions and then leave her alone to carry them out. Jeanne still claims to have been recognised as the fastest stringer of tomato plants in Newbourne.

One thing that Jeanne never mastered was driving. Her husband Arthur's first car was an old maroon Armstrong Siddeley Sapphire. He sat his test three times before passing, and then decided to teach Jeanne. Her first – and last – lesson involved driving down Jackson Road towards our house. With her not being able to see anything over the steering wheel, and applying the throttle instead of the brake, the car missed our 1,000-gallon water tank by inches. Arthur, in somewhat colourful language, instructed her to get out of the car. She gladly obeyed, and never drove again.

For many years, teenagers from Ipswich would cycle to Newbourne during their school holidays, offering their services to smallholders needing casual labour, particularly during the peak tomato season.

Most of those who helped us were boys, although one of the hardest workers was a stunning girl, Jane, on track to study at the Royal Academy of Dramatic Art. I remember idly wondering how the dust, burning heat and tomato tar would affect her flawless complexion. Having left home by that time, I only saw her very occasionally, which was rather sad.

One of the boys was Eddy Alcock, a pupil at Ipswich School. Eddy and his friend, John Cook, were taken on as tomato pickers by my father in about 1952. *"I remember toiling all day, breaking to consume our packed lunches and seeing our task as a never ending one, such was the immense length of those greenhouses and the abundance of the crop,"* said Eddy. *"I also remember – as we all do – when thinking back to our school days, the summer holiday was one of unbroken hot sunshine and not a drop of rain! It was hot in those greenhouses!"*

I imagine that hard work in Newbourne will have stood these

temporary labourers in good stead in later life. In Eddy's case, being trusted to work unsupervised was a new experience. *"I recall one occasion in particular, when Mr Belcham said that we would be all alone that day as he and his family were going sailing. Such was our pride in being trusted in this way that I think we worked harder than usual."* Eddy went on to pursue a successful career in civil engineering, serve a term as Chairman of Suffolk County Council, and receive an OBE for *"public and voluntary service in Suffolk"*.

Schoolboys (in grey flannel trousers!) at work on the Prop
(G Madgwick)

9 – BLOOD, TOIL, TEARS AND SWEAT

In May 1940, eight months into the Second World War, Winston Churchill addressed the nation. His message was summed up in those immortal words, *"I have nothing to offer but blood, toil, tears and sweat."*

Many of Newbourne's incoming tenants had already endured a six-month crash course in horticulture and stock-rearing. They had then had the back-breaking task of turning some generally poor agricultural land into productive smallholdings. So they may have been tempted to respond, *"What's new?"*

For several in Newbourne, the war will have been literally a time of blood and tears. At least one LSA family had someone in the armed services during that time. Mr and Mrs Ellis of 17 Mill Road are said to have received a telegram informing them that their son Jack was missing in action. They were greatly relieved to learn later that he was alive, having lost his right arm. Doubtless there were others. A memorial in the churchyard commemorates three from the village who died in the First World War, while an altar cross and two candlesticks commemorate the deaths of Owen Wolton in WW1 and Peter Wolton in WW2.

Patriotism was certainly not lacking. When hostilities began, some settlers, even those yet to complete their training, wanted to fight for their country. Such was their enthusiasm, LSA Head Office issued a circular pointing out that *"agriculture is a reserved occupation"* and that it was *"important that all not called up remain at their posts, especially those trained or nearly trained."* They also asked the government *"to treat all key staff on estates as reserved posts"*.

Two days before war was declared, another note from Head Office advised on the camouflaging of greenhouses: *"If camouflaging is carried out it must be in accordance with the specification of the ARP Dept of the Home Office, who suggest a coat of varnish sprayed with granite dust or green sand ... a contribution towards the cost may be made from public funds."* It's unclear whether this was ever done in Newbourne. The Madgwick's worked on the assumption that the acres of glass led the Germans to believe they were flying over water.

Camouflaging greenhouses was not uppermost in the mind of 14-year-old Ivy Griffiths. On 3rd September 1939, Ivy says she was helping plant mint on one of the smallholdings when someone called out that war had been declared. She dropped the plants and ran home, really upset. When her mother asked the reason, she said that she'd heard the Germans wanted *"blue-eyed blonde girls for stud purposes,"* and didn't leave the house for the rest of the week.

Our parents did their best to shield us from the unpleasant realities of war. I understand that the only German bomb to have dropped on Newbourne made a large crater close to the pumping station at the end of Fenn Lane, and often wonder whether that was the explosion my mother told me was *"Granny slamming the door"*! But I do remember the night sky swept by the criss-crossing beams of the searchlight battery above the pit at the foot of Hemley Hill. And I can still recall my father in his khaki battledress ready for Home Guard parade, as well as the crossed Union Jacks nailed above the greenhouse door on VE Day – or was it VJ Day?

There was great excitement when the crew of an American bomber baled out over Jackson Road. Even now I can picture the white parachutes heading straight for us as the plane continued its slow flight inland. We learned later that the parachutists had been horrified to discover that their landing site was not water but a sea of glass! My father was carrying a billy can of tea for the landgirls working on the holding when an airman landed in front of him between two rows of glass cloches. As the relieved man struggled to his feet, he was handed an enamel mug and told, *"You yanks think we're slow over here. Have a cup of tea!"*

I learned recently that the plane, a Flying Fortress, had been limping back to its base in Northamptonshire after a bombing raid in Germany, and crash-landed near Ipswich. We greatly appreciated the delivery of chewing gum and oranges a few days later by a high-ranking American officer. The full and moving story of this flight, including how the pilot risked his life to avoid crashing on to

Flying Fortress (Wikimedia Commons)

a factory in Ipswich – probably Cranes – is in Appendix B.

Other incidents recorded by the local police inspector include an incendiary bomb found near a straw stack in Newbourne in 1941; three members of a Halifax bomber crew baling out in 1942, two landing in Newbourne and one in Hemley; and an American Thunderbolt crash-landing at Church Farm in Waldringfield on 26th January 1944. In July 1944, an *"American 100lb aerial practice smoke bomb fell and exploded on Frost's Farm in Newbourn"*.

Two German airmen were killed and two captured when their Junkers 188 was shot down and crashed near Kirton Creek on 15th October 1943. All four had baled out, but two were already fatally injured. According to Richard Vickerstaff, one airman was eventually apprehended and taken to the home of Mrs Wicks, *"a Christian lady in Hemley"*. Florrie Wicks was certainly not overawed by the regular soldiers arriving at her house to make the arrest. *"Put those guns down,"* she said. *"He's someone's boy. Let him have his tea first."*

The story is confirmed by David Sterry of Hemley. David's father, George, helped locate the crashed plane for those who succeeded in digging it up in 1987, together with four unexploded bombs. Jeff Carless of the recovery team says, *"reports at the time concluded that at least part of the bomb load went up on impact. However, we all have serious doubts about that given the state and amount of wreckage found. Personally, I believe that there are still some 50kg*

The recovery team near Kirton Creek, 1987:
(L to R) Nigel Beckett, Jeff Carless, Ian Mclaclan, Bob Collis, David Wade and Clint Cansdale. (Jeff Carless)

bombs buried at the site. The wreckage and bombs were all found buried together." The full story of the recovery of the plane together with over thirty photos can be found at

www.flickr.com/photos/67251416@N08/sets/72157632850237870.

A police report in November 1943 also has *"Thomas Pickering, aged 16, of 48 Mill Road, injured by the explosion of a German ammunition round which he had been tampering with and which he found near the scene of the crash of Junkers 188."* Thomas was the son of the then Estate Manager, T R Pickering.

It seems that Florrie Wicks was not alone in providing for the needs of her enemy. Arthur "Nobby" Smith relates the story of another *"Christian lady"*, this time in Kirton. Early in the war a Messerschmitt 109 crash-landed close to the Falkenham Road, *"in Les Kemp's field near the Kirton Reading Room."* The plane had lost its fuel when the tank was ruptured by a bullet. Nobby met the pilot climbing over the fence out of the field. Unsurprisingly, conversation proved difficult, so Nobby took him home. While the pilot waited on the doorstep, Nobby told his mother that there was *"a man in uniform outside"*.

"Tell him to come in," she said.

With the young man enjoying a cup of his mother's tea *"and a wad"*, Nobby set off for the phone box.

"Mum's got a German pilot in the kitchen," he told local bobby PC Johnson. *"Please can you come and take him away."*

"No, I jolly well can't!" replied the officer.

Eventually the Felixstowe police arrived, and arrested the pilot. As they led him away, Nobby heard his mum, a staunch chapel-goer, call out, *"You look after him. He's some mother's son."*

Newbourne's Local Defence Volunteers were formed early in the war. Leading lights included Jimmy Jackson at No 10 Ipswich Road and Richard Vickerstaff at No 11. When Churchill became Prime Minster, he was concerned that the LDVs' name did not accurately reflect what he saw as a competent, professional fighting force, and had them renamed the Home Guard. According to Richard Vickerstaff Jnr, there was a certain time lag in Newbourne between the change of name and the development of anything resembling a *"professional fighting force"*.

In fact, Richard's description of Newbourne's Home Guard in its earliest days is strikingly similar to that of the Warmington-on-Sea Home Guard in the first episode of the BBC's *Dad's Army*. *"They only had one rifle between three people plus 5 rounds of ammunition,"* said Richard. *"Someone used all five rounds firing at a passing German plane, and was taken to task at the next parade."*

Any ill-discipline or disorder did not last for long. Newbourne's Captain Mainwaring was Joseph Causton of Brightwell Hall, who farmed the Brightwell Estate and was a director of the millers R W Paul. *"The Home Guard took things very seriously,"* remembers Georgie Madgwick, whose father was a sergeant. *"They used to have rifle practice in the crag pit on the road to Hemley. During the war, fetes were held on the field next to the Rectory, where the Home Guard did demonstrations with mortars."*

I heard recently that my father was involved in the capture of a German paratrooper. Whatever part this hapless airman was to have played in Hitler's plans to defeat Britain, it all came to nothing at the water mill. Whether his folding bike had brakes is not known, but, descending Mill Hill at high speed, he failed to negotiate the second bend and rode straight into the mill yard where he was promptly arrested.

As everywhere in Britain during the war, ARP (Air Raid Precaution) wardens in Newbourne were responsible for ensuring compliance with the blackout regulations. We all had to use blackout curtains at our windows to hide house lights from German bombers. Alf Chesher was a voluntary warden in Newbourne, and Ivy Griffiths remembers him gathering his team in the family kitchen on their duty night before checking all round the village for chinks of light.

Newbourne also had an Auxiliary Fire Service. *"All they seemed to do was get the engine out, polish it and put it back,"* said Richard Vickerstaff. *"They met on the central farm, and it was generally reckoned that their job was to keep the fires going until the professionals arrived!"* The professionals were men from the National Fire Service based in Felixstowe. They each had a uniform, hat and axe, and practised using the brook by Brook Cottage, helping the Dows water their garden.

Alec Jacobs has clear memories of the troops stationed in Kirton, where he still works at the forge. *"The sergeants' mess was opposite the forge,"* he says, *"but the big-wigs and all the transport were at Manor Farm."* He also remembers six-inch Howitzer guns at the

Maltings, where a new estate was recently built on the road to Trimley. Kirton Hall House was an officers' mess, with 25-pounder guns in Kirton Hall drive. There were anti-aircraft guns in the fields, searchlights in Park Lane, and in the fields of Manor Farm a red light, used as a beacon to guide air-craft.

Six-inch howitzer gun in the Royal Artillery Museum
(Max Smith, Wikimedia Commons)

Another officers' mess was in Burnt House Lane, and a cook house at the old village hall in Rectory Lane. All the transport was parked at top end of the green. On D-Day, Alec says all the vehicles had white stars painted on top for identification purposes.

Joan Cone started work at the Kirton Co-op in 1940. In one of the war stories on the BBC's history website, Joan wrote, *"About 250 soldiers were billeted in Kirton. They mostly slept in tents, and the church room became their mess hut."* She added that *"We had a good social life centred around the two village pubs, The Greyhound and The White Horse, specially if somebody played the piano. We had some good sing-songs, and sometimes we cleared a space to make room for dancing. We went to proper dances in Newbourne Village Hall. The soldiers took us in their trucks."*

(www.bbc.co.uk/history/ww2peopleswar/stories/47/a7138947.shtml)

As in other rural communities during the war, smaller families in Newbourne were expected to accommodate evacuee children. These were youngsters needing a safe environment away from their homes in the larger towns and cities that were prime targets for German bombers. Some host communities also housed evacuee families, but I have never heard of that being so in Newbourne. The Dow family at Brook Cottage had two children from the east end of London, who David Dow remembered had never seen a rabbit, let alone caught and eaten one! During the Spanish Civil War from 1936 to 1939, Britain welcomed 4,000 children evacuated from the Basque region. The Dows had also provided a home for two of these children, together

Evacuee children (Imperial War Museum)

with someone allocated as their teacher.

David, known as *"Dumpy Dow"* by his contemporaries, was still able to picture standing outside Brook Cottage with his brother, watching the searchlights on top of the bank on the other side of Woodbridge Road. *"One night we saw a Heinkel caught by a searchlight,"* he said. *"It was brought down somewhere near Rendlesham. I remember thinking 'How exciting if this is the war!'"*

John Hedley's parents, Alf and Ethel, were tenants at No. 2 Ipswich Road throughout the war. Along with other Newbourne children, John used to walk to school in Waldringfield. On one occasion, they were stopped by the police, who warned them not to touch any strange objects because the Germans had been dropping quantities of the so-called *"butterfly bomb"*. These small but lethal devices were designed to flutter gently to earth, and had three types of fuse. Some exploded on impact, some after a delay and some when touched. John doesn't recall any deaths or injuries, but adds, *"All Miss Stebbings, the headmistress, said was, 'You are late!'"*

John also remembers the British Army camp on the site of the present Foxhall waste disposal site. *"There must have been thousands of soldiers,"* he said. *"One day we decided to give it a look. The camp was a silent as the grave. We didn't know, of course, that D-Day was imminent."* John spoke, too, about German prisoners-of-war working in Newbourne. *"About 16 of them arrived each day on a lorry. They had no guards, just the lorry driver. They were so polite, too. Dad used to give them tomatoes and cucumbers, which they smuggled back to wherever they were based."* The POWs used to make model windmills as presents for his family, and would sometimes sit him on their laps – all a bit ironic, really, when their colleagues were dropping butterfly bombs less than a mile away.

In September 1944, Georgie Madgwick watched some of the gliders flying overhead en route to Arnhem. *"The sky was black with them,"* he said. While Newbourne was never likely to be one of Hitler's prime targets, it was on the path of his V1 flying bombs or *"doodlebugs"*. These were directed primarily at London, and, at their peak, arrived at a rate of over 100 every day. Their engines were designed to cut out over their intended target, but were notoriously unreliable. If the engine noise overhead stopped suddenly, those under the flight path would hold their breath and wait for the inevitable explosion. Although the under-stairs cupboard in Georgie's home had been strengthened to provide protection for just such occasions, his mother more often than not just froze in the middle of the room. She would simply clutch her children to her and hope for the best! The Cheshers opposite had built their own air raid shelter.

The proximity of Martlesham Heath aerodrome provided us youngsters with plenty of interest. From 1917 until 1939 the airfield had seen a lot of experimental work. But once hostilities began, this was moved away to the relative safety of Boscombe Down in Wiltshire. Throughout the war Martlesham Heath was a fighter station, initially under the auspices of the RAF and then, from 1943, the USAAF. The RAF flew Blenheim bombers, Spitfires, Hurricanes and Typhoons. The Americans flew Thunderbolts and Mustangs.

In 1945, the aerodrome was returned to the RAF, who used it for a variety of experiments with planes and ammunition until its closure in 1963. They flew Meteor jets from there in the 1950s, and also pursued development of the autogyro.

My brother Michael recalls a small passenger plane, the De Havilland Devon/Dove, often circling continuously above our house during the early 50s. He was later told by one of the Martlesham Heath boffins that they were trialling an automatic landing system. This involved the plane doing *"bumps"* – that is, taking off, circling, landing, taking off, etc. Of course, a pilot would always be on board even when flying totally on automatic in case of emergency.

During one of their early experiments the control tower had brought the plane in to a trouble-free landing. But then there was a bit of a mix-up in communications. The pilot didn't think that another flight was planned and got out. Those in the control tower thought otherwise and the plane took off again with no pilot aboard.

Horrified, the pilot ran for the control tower. A senior officer saw what had happened and stopped him half way up the steps. He didn't want the operator knowing that he was effectively flying the first *"solo"* flight and that there was no back up if he got anything wrong! He got quite a shock when the pilot walked in just after he had brought it in to land!

The aerodrome had been out of bounds to the public throughout the war. But security must have been relaxed considerably after the war ended because a friend, John Aldous, and I soon discovered at least one unguarded dump of aircraft bits and pieces close to the southern perimeter. For boys not yet in their teens, being able to clamber into discarded cockpits, complete with instrument panels, was

bliss. We poked and prodded various bits and pieces lying nearby. None of them exploded but I suppose they could have done.

The noise of aircraft, British and American, was very much a part of our upbringing. The distinctive sounds of Spitfire and Meteor were as

Spitfires (Wikimedia Commons)

familiar to us as the nightingale and cuckoo. Later, as teenagers in the 1950s on the river at Waldringfield, the silence was regularly broken by pairs of USAAF Thunderstreaks, Sabres and Thunderjets flying sorties from Bentwaters and Woodbridge airfields. Sometimes we saw one of the much quieter seaplanes and flying boats based at RAF Felixstowe.

An enduring memory of the war is finding countless narrow strips of silver foil, each only a few inches long, scattered across one of the fields farmed by Harry Bater from Bucklesham Hall. It must have been towards the end of the war, and I was told by my parents that this was *"window"*, used by both the RAF and the Luftwaffe to confuse enemy radar during bombing raids. History records that it was very effective in doing so, as well as for decorating our family Christmas tree.

Eventually, the blood, toil, tears and sweat were over. So was the unpopular British Double Summer Time, when clocks were put forward two hours each summer to make the most of the daylight. Peace at last. Newbourne rejoiced. Life would soon return to normal. It had been a long, hard and painful slog, but everyone knew the alternative would have been infinitely worse.

Many years later and far from Newbourne, something must have prompted my mother to look back on the dark days of war with a hint of nostalgia. When she died in 1998, we found the following among several poems she had written. I had the privilege of reading it at her thanksgiving service.

WE LIVED IN PEACE …

Yesterday – or so it seems! –
We lived in peace, had time for dreams.
Able to wander, breathe Suffolk air
Clean and fresh. We'd time to spare.
In '43 and '44,
We lived in peace – but were at war!!

Fighters and bombers overhead
Defended freedom, so 'twas said.
Fought to defend our precious peace,
Which we'd regain once war would cease!

Children below trod woods and lanes,
Disregarding threatening planes;
Filling childhood's endless days
With streams and birds in flower-filled ways.
While our bombers overhead
Filled other hearts than ours with dread.

Now, through Suffolk's lovely skies
A screaming US aircraft flies!
Carrying sinister, lethal loads,
While down below, huge concrete roads
Criss-crossing Suffolk, swift and new,
Bearing endless traffic through
From industry to busy dock! –
I know one can't put back the clock –

But oh! I wish, before I die
That I could hear the curlew cry!
Pick bluebells in a Suffolk lane,
Undisturbed by a screaming 'plane.
Once more I'd know sweet peace again
'Neath an empty Suffolk sky! ...

We lived in peace and now are "free",
It has a hollow ring for me!

Free! - huh!...

... "Trespassers will be prosecuted!
Don't drink the water, it's polluted!
You may not pick the sweet wild flower!
You can't park there more than an hour!
Keep your dog upon a lead,
Don't let him obey his natural need!
If he does then scoop the lot,
And take it home or you'll be shot!"

Free! - huh!

© Dorrie Belcham

10 – MAKE DO AND MEND

I can see it clearly even now. A threshing machine stands idle in the corner of the field. Several men are sitting on sheaves of barley, resting their backs against a stack of straw bales. Others, pitchforks beside them, lean against the wheels of a trailer piled high with sheaves yet to be threshed. The men are having their 'levenses – bread, cheese, tomatoes, and cold tea in a Camp Coffee bottle.

Similar scenarios were once played out across Suffolk towards the end of every summer. During the war, and possibly for several years afterwards, it was played out on our smallholding. My father grew barley in the field behind our piggery, and it was always threshed in the top corner nearest Sandy Lane.

The men wore flat caps. One – the foreman – may have had a Trilby. With sweat glistening, they were covered in chaff and dust. Trousers were held up either by braces or binder twine, with more twine tied tightly below the knee to keep out curious rats and mice. Most had waistcoats and rolled-up shirtsleeves.

What these men wore for a hard day's work is striking. Shirts had no collars – just holes for studs to secure detachable starched collars on formal occasions. Fabric used for waistcoats, jackets and trousers, while not always matching, was good quality. Footwear, if not army boots, was leather, worn and unpolished but stylish. Headgear had probably been bought originally for Sunday best.

Those were times of *"make do and mend"*. Few could afford clothes designed purely for work. Young or old, we just used our worn-out best clothes. Before the days of man-made fibre, at least they were warm and durable. Worn bits were patched. Holes in sweaters and socks were darned. John Hedley's father repaired John's school boots with bits of car or bicycle tyre. Mothers made clothes for their children, and taught those skills to their daughters. Sometimes they unpicked old sweaters and used the wool to knit balaclavas. Grannies knitted socks, gloves and scarves as Christmas and birthday presents. Clothes were handed down to the next in line, or even the next generation – I started work as an apprentice, wearing the suit my father had worn for his wedding (and with the bike he had used when he was courting!).

Shopping was something mothers did. Men worked long hours on the holdings providing for their families. They looked to their wives for clean clothes, meals on the table, and the children kitted out for school. But it was not easy, at least at our end of Jackson Road. Shopping in Ipswich took a full morning or afternoon, beginning and ending with a half-mile walk along an often muddy Sandy Lane. With early closing each Wednesday, no Sunday opening, no cash machines and no supermarkets, it was anything but a pleasure. For some years, my mother shopped in Felixstowe. This meant cycling to Kirton, leaving her bike at the forge, and catching the bus through Falkenham and Trimley. Coming down Mill Hill on the way home, tired and with a fully-laden bicycle, would not have been much fun.

A year or two after the LSA arrived in Newbourne, the post office was run by Mr and Mrs Eagle. This was part of their shop in what is now the Red House, just past the entrance to Street Farm. Mary Sharland helped out there in her early teens. Georgie Madgwick always knew when Mildred Eagle was angry or upset, as she could be heard from his father's holding in Mill Road. When we arrived in 1942, the post office was at No 23 Mill Road, and run by Mr and Mrs Escritt. They later built the bungalow on Stocks Corner next to the church, and ran the post office from there. The bungalow was a proper corner shop as well, but at No 23 we had only been able to buy stamps and postal orders. Jeanne Gilder says she had to cycle to Marks' shop in Bucklesham to buy cigarettes. Now demolished, Marks was opposite Holly Lane, known then as Hulver Lane (*"hulver"* being the Suffolk word for holly).

Mercifully, many supplies were brought direct to the door, especially in the early days. *"Most food that was not grown was delivered,"* remembers Ivy Griffiths, adding that *"Mrs Cornell and, later, Hughie Cornell, would fill a milk jug if left on the doorstep."* At some stage, Hughie brought milk to us in bottles from Kembroke Hall on the back of his bike. *"Then the Co-op got in on the act,"* says Ivy, *"and brought milk, bread, groceries and meat. They were very reliable: order one week, deliver the next."* Mr Pask, the Felixstowe butcher, delivered meat. A fishmonger from somewhere called from time to time. Mr Spurgeon, who preceded the Daveys at the shop in Waldringfield, baked and delivered bread. Early on, *"the oilman"* brought paraffin. Jeanne Gilder recalls deliveries from Mr Roe, who had a shop at Kirton. Bertie Bell from Waldringfield delivered our

greengrocery for many years. Ice cream was made in-house, initially by mixing custard with snow, but it was eventually delivered by Peter's. The arrival of their van was heralded by a tinny rendering of *Greensleeves* or similar, which rather spoiled the weekend peace and quiet and annoyed my father intensely. He eventually forbade the van turning in our drive, so the driver had to turn next door. Bundles of the *Evening Star* left Ipswich at 4.30pm on the 232 bus and were thrown unceremoniously into the bus shelter opposite the Fox.

Washing – clothes, dishes, pots, pans, and small children – was also what mothers did. To start with, my mother did it all – including babies – in the large Belfast sink in the kitchen. Laundry and washing up were both done with powders like Oxydol, Omo, Rinso and Persil. Something called Reckitt's Blue was used for whitening the clothes. For many years the family wash was done without a washing machine, spin dryer or tumble dryer. A wringer removed the worst of the water, the wind did the rest. A clothes horse in front of the range finished the process – finishing it completely on one occasion, when everything went up in flames. Us older children were expected to help with drying up, with our father tending to do the washing up at weekends.

We had one bath a week, for which we used Lifebuoy red carbolic soap, and had to clean our school shoes every day. Our hair was cut by Arthur Locke in a shed near his house. One day he was called away, leaving me to experiment with the clippers. I cut away a large chunk at the front of my head. I can't recall who had to explain things to my parents – and whether he still charged the usual 6d. Once at school in Ipswich, our hair was cut by Wootons in Tavern Street.

When mothers were not shopping, washing, mending, attending to children, or helping on the holding, they were cooking. The kitchen was our mother's territory in our house. Early on, the only electrical kitchen appliances were the GEC Magnet cooker with solid plates, and a shiny copper electric kettle. With no fridge or freezer, keeping food fresh and protected from bugs was difficult. Eggs could be preserved for cooking purposes for up to a year in isinglass. Fruit was bottled in Kilner jars or made into jam. Seville oranges, when available, were turned into marmalade; an exploding pressure cooker once plastered a vast quantity across the kitchen ceiling. Part of a pig was hung, salted, in the under-stairs cupboard. Meat was kept in a meat safe in the pantry.

Flies were plentiful because of livestock. Sticky flypapers adorned our kitchen and dining room, and a muslin curtain across the back door kept wasps and flies at bay. Wasps were also trapped in water-filled jam jars, with a jam-smeared hole in the lid. Finding and destroying wasp nests needed two people. One held a wasp gently against the window pane, while the other tied a length of cotton around its neck. Finding the nest was simply a matter of following the cotton. Headless wasps, unlike chickens, can't fly, so correctly tensioning the cotton was important. Hornets were rare. The only nest we knew of was in an alder tree the other side of the valley. We always gave it a wide berth.

Not all our food was purchased or home-grown. Pheasants and partridges were shot in season, and rabbits shot or snared year-round. For some reason, pigeons did not feature. Until the early fifties, rabbits were plentiful. At harvest, as the binders circled a field, rabbits were forced into the steadily diminishing area of standing corn. Boys like us, each brandishing *"a grut ole stoone"*, would spot them crouching low between the rows, and dispatch them quickly with a *"good ole clout on th' hid."* Those making a break for it (rabbits, not boys) were shot, and the spoils shared at the end of the day. David

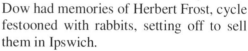

Dow had memories of Herbert Frost, cycle festooned with rabbits, setting off to sell them in Ipswich.

Between 1953 and 1955 the vile disease, myxomatosis, is thought to have wiped out 95% of the UK's rabbits. On our way to and from the bus to school, we often found these blinded creatures trapped in Sandy Lane, too weak to climb the steep banks. We were glad to put them out of their misery with a smart blow with a stick across the back of their necks.

Blackberries from our hedge, apples and plums from the orchard, yellow bullace plums for jam from the other side of the valley, sweet chestnuts for roasting at Christmas, and mushrooms from the meadow, were all enjoyed in season. Mrs Lucking taught us how to identify watercress in the little stream. I think she came from Waldringfield, and had the gift of dowsing.

"There was no obesity then," says Georgie Madgwick. Georgie spoke of his mother, Hannah, using a large pan on the cooker for cooking everything from soup and dumplings to the Geordie favourite, pease pudding. It was also used for boiling pigs' heads and trotters for brawn, and was not always emptied of its contents before a new dish was prepared. *"She also did the washing in it,"* insisted Georgie. His wife, Cynthia, was horrified.

With money tight, and some rationing not ending until 1954, our diet was restricted. As children, we had never known anything different, so took it for granted that one slice of plain bread and butter was to be eaten at teatime before anything with jam – or the wonderful honey that came in huge drums from Mr Gordon at Debenham. Marmite or Bovril were  acceptable alternatives on the first slice but I hated both. Bloater paste was just about okay. When sweets were available, a Mars Bar, a real treat, was sliced and shared between us. I realised that not all children were as well provided for when a girl brought something to eat in the den we were making. It was sugar and margarine smeared on a piece of bread.

Breakfasts always included bacon, fried bread, eggs and tomatoes, as well as Farmer's Glory Wheatflakes, Welgar Shredded Wheat, bread and milk or barley flakes. Porridge was another of my dislikes. We drank milk both at home and at school. I don't think we drank tea until our teens. The only *"coffee"* available was Camp Coffee, made from chicory essence. It smelled quite unlike the coffee beans always roasting in a revolving drum in the window of Limmer's restaurant in Ipswich.

For many years, the main meal was at midday. This was school lunch during term time, but at other times our mother's cooking kept us warm and full of energy. We always seemed to have enough meat, although I suspect that her portions were always smaller than ours. Vegetables were plentiful, but were definitely not cooked *al dente*! As for *"afters"*, she always knew our favourites: syrup, chocolate and jam sponge puddings or blackberry and apple pie, all with oodles of custard; rice puddings or, even better, really creamy barley puddings. *"I bags the skin,"* we'd cry almost before any of it reached the table.

Cycles, like clothes, were passed down. As the eldest child, I had the first tricycle and the first bike. These were duly passed to Michael and Jeremy only after I had covered them in dents and scratches.

 Cameras and other luxury goods were few and far between. My father had a camera, and I got hold of a Box Brownie in my late teens. *"I remember the Americans being at Bentwaters,"* says Sue Whittaker, who lived at 23 Mill Road. *"There was a girl from there in my class at the convent when I was 5. She seemed very exotic with her American accent. Her dad had a camera that took colour pictures. We only had black and white."*

We never talked of DIY, probably because *"doing it yourself"* was a way of life. If our parents wanted something, it was usually a matter of making it themselves from whatever was to hand. And they taught us to do the same. All painting and decorating, most car, cycle and toy repairs, and most construction and renovation work around the holding was done in-house. For anything more complicated, Arthur Gilder was summoned.

Medical attention was fairly rudimentary. Our doctors included Dr Hider or Hyder from Ipswich, and Drs Guiver and Dawney from Woodbridge. Barry Gilder remembers Dr Dawney as a shy man, who held a surgery in the Village Hall each Thursday, and wore tweeds, brown brogues and a hat. Our dentist in the early days was John Payne-James in Ipswich. I recall having nine milk teeth removed in under two minutes while laid out with some kind of gas, and spitting out large quantities of blood travelling home on the bus.

Colds meant bed with a hot water bottle. The usual childhood infections like measles happened. Michael had bronchitis. My father was confined to bed with a duodenal ulcer very soon after we arrived, and in 1948 my mother was laid up for some months with a bug from infected meat. It was so serious that an antidote had to be obtained from Calcutta before she regained her health. We three brothers were sent to stay with relatives for the duration, and Michael and I had to attend different schools. On our return, we found that our parents had gone vegetarian. We were introduced to such delights as nut rissoles and unsweetened lemon juice, while our coughs were treated with a foul-smelling herbal mixture called Liquafruta. One of us managed to smash a bottle in the school cloakroom, and was not popular. We became very healthy and very thin, with Michael looking like a skeleton. The regime was eventually abandoned.

The winter of 1947 was exceptionally severe, and lasted for several months. The only heating I remember at that time was the range in the dining room, and an open fire in the sitting room. The range provided us with hot water. Ice obscured the single-glazed Crittal windows as we got up each morning. We used to make peep-holes in the wonderful fern-like patterns using heated pennies. Short trousers and long socks, all made of wool, kept us warm. No fitted carpets, of course – just rugs on cold lino. The sitting room had a standard nine-foot by twelve-foot carpet in the centre, with exposed floorboards all round, stained black. No wallpaper, either. For many years, all walls were coated in distemper and ceilings in whitewash.

All in all, it was tough then, especially for anyone who was a parent. We were too young, of course, to realise, and just accepted life as it was.

Unsurprisingly, play could be tough, too. But that merits a chapter of its own.

11 – OUT TO PLAY

What a wonderful playground we had – and all on our doorstep! Across the road lay meadows, woods and streams. At the end of the road was an overgrown orchard. Less than a hundred yards up Sandy Lane were two disused crag pits. Trees of all shapes and sizes surrounded us, and we were allowed to climb them all. We built dens wherever we chose, and could shout at the top of our voices whenever the mood took us.

Traffic was minimal, so our back yard, drive and the road were all available. Lorry and tractor drivers quickly learned to anticipate younger children learning to ride bikes, as well as older children pushing one another on a variety of more experimental vehicles, best described as boxes on wheels.

Accidents did happen, of course. A smaller box on wheels was used for the wooden bricks we played with as toddlers. When I let it run down the corrugated iron roof of the lean-to, my brother Michael, who was sitting on the ground below, was fortunate only to receive a nasty gash on the head. Michael must have been a bit accident-prone. He once got another bang on the head in the same lean-to. When trying to weigh himself using a heavy sack balance, the nail from which it hung gave way.

Again, it was Michael who had the most serious cycle accident when his front wheel hit part of a tractor lying in Mill Road. And it was Michael we rolled down the almost vertical side of the big pit in a 40-gallon oil drum, straight into an oak tree. My brother Jeremy and I both had falls, with scars still evident today. We were clearly foolish to

attempt cycling to school down Grove Lane hill in Ipswich without holding the handlebars, but we lived to tell the tale.

Our own toboggan slope was on the other side of the big stream. It was fun to start with but, as we grew older, we headed for Christchurch Park in Ipswich when it snowed. The slope there was crowded, and often strewn with bits of broken sledge. Older youngsters would hurtle down, four or more on a sledge, and woe betide anyone in their way! Our home-made wooden effort was totally inadequate, so our father had one welded together from galvanised water pipe at the forge in Kirton. It – and we – survived unscathed. The toboggan is now used by Jeremy's grandchildren.

We built up a wonderful arsenal of weapons, some of which could easily have caused serious injury. As cowboys, we produced realistic bangs with cap pistols, modelled on the revolvers we saw in comics and films. Louder bangs could be produced by pushing the red head of a Swan Vestas match into a hollow padlock key using a blunt nail, and bashing the nail with a hammer or against a wall. The best explosions of all needed ingredients – including earplugs – easily obtainable from a chemist. Itching powder could be made from rose hips.

Michael

As Indians, we made our own bows from hazel shoots and tomato string; arrows were bamboo canes, split to take cardboard flights. Pop guns were really only rudimentary air guns firing a cork on a string, and were soon superseded by the superior home-made version. These fired acorns at high velocity from pieces of elder branch from which the pith had been removed.

Other weapons included catapults, usually home-made from wood, and, for a brief while, quarterstaffs inspired by the Errol Flynn film, *Robin Hood*. We all had penknives, and, although not allowed them ourselves, some primary school friends wore sheath knives on their belts. These were sharpened on the school's spit-moistened concrete window sills. Stabbings were unheard of.

Best of all were the throwing arrows. Three-foot bamboo canes had cardboard flights fitted to one end and a nail to the other. If they had hit anyone, it would have been a hospital job. One end of a four-foot piece of string was held in a quick-release half-hitch on a small nail just below the flights; the other was wrapped around the hand holding the arrow near its tip. Throwing it like a javelin, with the string adding impetus, 100-yard distances were easily achievable. Accuracy was rubbish.

The worst accident by far was the death of my friend John Aldous in a sandpit on Brook Hill in Kirton. John was apparently digging a tunnel when it collapsed. Other potentially serious incidents included my fall from a tree while collecting jackdaw eggs, and landing on my back on a log. Our friend Christopher Cracknell survived several nasty accidents. He once fell from a piggery roof and was only saved from disaster when his shorts caught on a nail, leaving him suspended in mid-air. His father dragged him in the nick of time from a 40-gallon drum half full of water into which he had fallen head first. And he was also extremely fortunate not to have suffered any long-term injury when he thrust his arm into a rabbit hole, and withdrew it firmly clamped in a gin trap. Michael had to run home to find our father, who freed the trapped arm. Christopher was not someone who cried easily, and he didn't on that occasion. Michael tells of being with Christopher when his father, Harry, chased them up the holding wielding a strap that was always kept on the back of their bathroom door. Perhaps he was accustomed to pain?

Some mishaps were more amusing than serious. Georgie Madgwick and Alan Roberts were exploring the partially-built post office and shop near the church, when one of them stuck his foot through the ceiling. Michael was playing darts in the Village Hall using a board hanging behind the door. Barry Gilder opened the door and received a dart in his arm. Heavy usage had turned the point of the dart into a hook, so extracting it was not easy. When Barry fell into the big stream during the winter, sister Lindy dutifully removed all his wet clothes and wheeled him home on her bike. Sadly, no-one took a photo. My father fell into the big stream in his best suit while trying to get a better view of a robin's nest. Jeremy set fire to a felled oak tree with a magnifying glass just before getting on the school bus at the top of Sandy Lane. Coming home later, he found that much had been burned away. The remains, including charred wood, are still there.

Trying to improve the reception on his grandfather's old wireless set almost led to disaster for Michael. He was in bed suffering from a bad back, and decided to connect the aerial to the bedsprings. When my mother applied Elliman's Embrocation to his back she got a bit of a shock, although not as bad as my father got when he checked out the problem using foil from a chocolate bar!

When we arrived in Newbourne, the Colmers lived at No. 16 Ipswich Road. This was opposite the top of Sandy Lane, where as older children we used to wait for the bus into Ipswich for school. Mr Colmer never seemed very friendly, and the burning oak tree probably didn't help. Things really went downhill after Michael inserted a lit banger into the end of a long piece of dried cow parsley and hurled it through Mr C's open sitting room window. The bus arrived just in time.

Our collective recollection is that we were never at a loose end, although this is not entirely borne out by Michael's entry in his special *"Coronation Diary"*: *"Played with kittens, got bored, played with kittens some more, walked about, got bored....."*. Lindy and Barry Gilder used to take sandwiches down to the woods for the whole day. *"No-one knew where we were,"* says Lindy. Unlike today – Lindy's mother, Jeanne, complains that her great-grandchildren have to phone home every 15 minutes. Barry prided himself on being pig rodeo champion, competing against Roger Salter, and has memories of walking round the churchyard late at night, trying to imagine the route of the tunnel rumoured to run between the church and Newbourne Hall. John Hedley says, *"We were free as birds, running through Primrose Wood, clothes off and swimming in the stream."*

Sue Whittaker remembers *"hop-scotch in the road, a pogostick, skipping, throwing a ball over the house and against the wall, rolling across the lawn in a 10-gallon drum, walks to the Springs to pick snowdrops, walks to the top of Jackson*

Young Farmers' Club visit to Surrey nursery in 1949. From left: Back row: Dennis Abbott, Ralf Johnson, Alan Roberts, nursery manager, Derek Cooley, Georgie Madgwick, Bertie Langley. Front row: Unknown, Laurie Sample, Laura Ross-Smith (G Madgwick)

Road to pick bluebells, riding my bike to Waldringfield, and the Young Farmers' Club in the hut." She adds: *"We went to school with Pauline, Charlotte and Tessa Somerville on the bus so we knew the family well. I used to go and play with Pauline at Newbourne Hall. I remember the bedrooms having sloping floors. Stuart Somerville, their father, wouldn't let us children into his studio – he was an artist."*

Jeremy was always the most interested and knowledgeable of us three about the natural world that surrounded us. As a toddler he could tell the difference between mushrooms and what he called *"doadills"* just by their smell. He was always digging up sharks' teeth from the crag pits and shards of mediaeval pottery from the orchard. Even now he remembers *"listening to the barn owls quartering the meadows at dusk, and shouting at the nightingales at night for singing too loud."* What none of us knew until recently, however, is that puddingpokes are long-tailed tits, *poke* being the Suffolk word for bag and their nests reminiscent of the bags in which puddings were made. Puddingpokes is also the area between Newbourne and Hemley behind No. 19 Mill Road.

Apart from the usual cats, which my father unceremoniously chased from the house if they ever ventured inside, pets included rabbits in hutches, tadpoles and sticklebacks in jam jars, and a jackdaw that would sit on my shoulder. For a brief while we had a black Labrador. Unwanted kittens – and that was most of them – were put in a sack immediately after birth and drowned in a bucket.

When very young, we shared our adventures with Diana "Dinks" and Christopher "Kiffy" Cracknell from No. 40 Jackson Road. When they moved to No. 17 Mill Road, No. 40 became home to Tony Pridham and later, I think, to Anthony Newbold, one of whom had a wonderful collection of Dinky toys and an army of lead soldiers.

I don't recall a youth or children's club, although Michael remembers an attempt to start a Scout group, which closed after one meeting. There was no cafe, coffee bar or chip shop within seven or eight miles. And no bus shelter to congregate in. Money, too, was in short supply. *"I remember saving 1s 9d for a money box,"* says Michael, *"and then the agony of not having anything left to put in it!"*

Deprived? I don't think so. Lindy Gilder summed it up well. *"We had the most wonderful childhood. We didn't have much; we were poor but we were safe. I look back on my childhood and think how lucky we were."*

12 – SPARE TIME

Earning a living from the land can be difficult to combine with an active social life. Wisely, the LSA saw the value of at least some leisure time for its tenants, and made its estate managers responsible for securing suitable social opportunities for them, their wives and children.

This was especially important during an estate's early years, when whole families faced life in an unfamiliar environment. They also had to get along with a native population who initially viewed them with a degree of suspicion. In the March 1961 *East Anglian Magazine*, Walter Tye commented on social life in Newbourne soon after the LSA arrived. *"Even organised meetings and lectures had but little effect. They continued to stare at one another from opposite sides of the newly erected community hut. From all accounts, it was the Fox Inn that eventually did most to break down the barriers that divided them."*

The estate manager, perhaps understandably, was much more upbeat in one of his first memos to Head Office: *"A Social Committee has been appointed, with some type of entertainment most evenings (including trips to Felixstowe for 'wives and kiddies')."* He also mentioned *"Whit Monday sports on the Rectory field."*

The *"newly erected community hut"* behind the Hall, as we saw in an earlier chapter, also doubled as a primary school during the war. In 1942 or thereabouts, community events as well as a doctor's surgery were moved for a time to Newbourne Hall, but – probably when the army took over the Hall – these were eventually based in a new building on the site of the present village hall.

According to Jeanne Gilder, this new facility was very small, and eventually burned down in the early 1960s. Its replacement, on the same site, arrived on the back of a lorry as a *"flat-pack"* from a farm in Stratford St Mary. Jeanne's husband Arthur, son Barry, and several others, erected and painted this new hut, incorporating that part of the former building which was still serviceable. Later, Arthur added a kitchen.

From the late 14th or early 15th Century, the Fox Inn had always been the hub of social life in Newbourne. When the population more than doubled with the arrival of the LSA, landlord Henry Hill and the

Tolly Cobbold brewery must have been delighted. The Fox quickly became the place for tenants to hear the latest gossip and enjoy Suffolk or Geordie humour. Sometimes it was somewhere to share – and drown – their sorrows. On most evenings, once Henry had called *"Time, gentlemen, please!"* (and sometimes much later), these men would return to their families, usually on foot or bicycle. Some were incapable of doing so, according to Ivy Griffiths. *"At least one was taken home in a wheelbarrow."*

Ivy's family was teetotal. *"Our parents never went to the Fox,"* she says, *"and us children were brought up in the same way. We always had to be in by 9.00pm."* She maintained that this meant the money they would have spent on drink was spent instead on clothes and other things, adding that *"many American GIs were in the area later on, and two girls fell pregnant."* Until Ivy started nursing, she had never been out after 9.00pm.

A youth club met in Newbourne Hall early in the war, while the Young Farmers' Club was formed soon afterwards. I remember my mother going to the Women's Institute. The Woodbridge Excelsior Band had players from Newbourne – Ernie Frost and Wally Hammond to name but two. *"Wonderful plays and concerts in the Village Hall"*

"Wonderful plays and concerts" (Roger Salter)

80

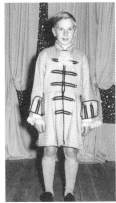

Above: From left - Mary Ruffle, Lindy Gilder, Pauline Mann (Jeanne Gilder). *Right: Alan Madgwick* (G Madgwick)

are remembered fondly by Jeanne Gilder. She recalls Miss Odwell, who lived in Little Cottage next to the chapel, writing and producing plays as well as making all the costumes. Kath Atack, wife of Jack Atack, the estate stores manager, made costumes for village theatrical performances. She also made them for the Black and White Minstrels, one of whom was married to their daughter Jean. The Atacks lived for a long while at No. 49 Fenn Lane.

The Christmas party in the former village hall was something we children always looked forward to. Strips of coloured paper were glued and made into paper chains, while our mothers produced oodles of jelly and brightly-coloured iced buns. With no artificial Christmas trees available at the end of the war, and no possibility of buying a real one, my enterprising father always made the tree. As he did for our Christmas tree at home, he would construct a framework of straight hazel shoots at right-angles to a thicker trunk. Looking rather like the mast of a square-rigged ship, this would then have small conifer branches wired to it, cut from a tree in the woodland below our holding. The result was amazingly realistic, and could support any number of heavy presents as well as the clip-on candle holders.

Most children's parties in the village hall seemed to feature a conjurer. I always tried to emulate their tricks at home, but with little success. In spite of avidly reading books on *"magic"* and practising hard, I was never booked for a performance other than by my long-suffering family. My party piece of turning water into wine, and then

81

wine back into water, was only possible because small boys could purchase potassium permanganate and hydrogen peroxide from chemists with no questions asked!

Few who could be called celebrities found their way to Newbourne. One who did was radio personality Percy Edwards. Percy lived in Ipswich, and performed at least twice in the village hall in the 1950s. He found us country folk a most appreciative audience. His ability to reproduce not only the calls of the birds and animals he loved so much but also the sound of my mother's Pfaff sewing machine was uncanny. Needless to say, I spent hours afterwards trying to do the same, but, like most boys, never got beyond blowing through cupped hands to sound like an owl. We were very fortunate to have him so accessible. When he died in 1996, the broadcaster and journalist Denis Gifford wrote in his obituary in *The Independent*, *"without a doubt Percy Edwards was the finest animal and bird impressionist British show-business ever knew."*

Another well-known local man was Sir Lawrence Bragg, joint winner with his father of the Nobel Prize for Physics. Sir Lawrence, who lived at *Quietways* in School Lane, Waldringfield, kept us entertained one evening in Waldringfield village hall when he demonstrated the mechanism of human speech. As an aspiring young inventor, I was enthralled by the voice-like sounds he was able to create using a collection of what looked liked nothing more than bellows, tubes and bits of leather and wood.

Sir Lawrence Bragg (A) in impressive company at a 1927 conference on quantum mechanics: Max Planck (B), Marie Curie (C), Albert Einstein (D)

Entertainment of a more professional standard was to be found in Ipswich. The first film I ever saw was at the Gaumont cinema – nowadays the Regent theatre. *Song of the South*, with Uncle Remus, Brer Rabbit and Brer Fox as its main characters, was eventually recognised as patronising towards African Americans, and Disney Enterprises decided not to release the film on home video in the United States. Whether the film implanted a sub-conscious racism in me or anyone else, it's impossible to say. But children in the forties and fifties did encounter blatant racist attitudes that would horrify most of us today. When 5-year-old Sue Whittaker's grandmother visited, *"an Indian man wearing a turban walked up the path. Gran told me to 'hide from the nasty black man'!"*

Social pressures have changed much that we took for granted as children. Undoubtedly, most of that change has been for the good. We really looked forward to the circus in Christchurch Park in Ipswich, but many of us now would totally oppose the caging of the wild animals that were obliged to perform for us.

Do we sometimes go too far, though? The Christmas pantomime at the Ipswich Hippodrome is sadly no more. It was always a not-to-be-missed occasion for our family and many others in Newbourne. We particularly enjoyed scrabbling under our seats for the sweets traditionally thrown into the audience, usually by the Dame. However, in December 2006 the *London Evening Standard* reported that *"bureaucrats are set to stamp out the tradition because they claim boiled sweets could injure a member of the audience"*. Instead, organisers of one pantomime were told they must go down into the crowd and hand out the sweets. The ruling was made because of fears an injury could spark a compensation claim.

As rock 'n' roll came to the fore in the late fifties, the coolest cats flocked to the Gondolier in Upper Brook Street, Ipswich's first espresso coffee bar. For the less cool, it was the Milk Bar in the Old Cattle Market. Neither school nor parents allowed us to join either group, and we gave any Teddy Boys a wide berth. If our parents were not hogging our new Dansette record player to listen to Mendelssohn's *Violin Concerto* or Beethoven's *Pastoral*, we played Bill Haley's *Rock around the clock*, singing along with him and his Comets. When *Rock around the clock* was featured in the film, *Blackboard jungle*, rampaging Teddy Boys nationwide ripped up cinema seats and jived in the aisles. A report of this happening at the Ipswich Gaumont was greeted in our house with incomprehension and much tut-tutting.

While rock 'n' roll had to cope with a generally bad press, skiffle gained in popularity. Money was a factor. Only needing to cover the cost of an acoustic guitar and perhaps a harmonica, a few friends were easily able to establish a group. Find a washboard, make a double base from a tea chest, broom handle and leather bootlace, and you had all you needed. Musical ability appeared to be less important than a passable American accent. My brother Michael and several of his classmates formed a group that played regularly at the Tuddenham Fountain and the Grundisburgh Half Moon. Not musical myself, I was content to impersonate skiffle legend Lonnie Donegan, to whom I was supposed to bear a resemblance, singing *Rock Island Line* and *Don't you rock me, daddy-o* down Sandy Lane.

Radio Luxemburg, *"The Station of the Stars"*, was essential listening in Newbourne long before Radio Caroline. Caroline, the most famous pirate radio station, began broadcasting pop music in 1964 from a lightship just outside British territorial waters off the Essex coast. I was not that interested in either, but as a family we occasionally bought one of the new 45-rpm vinyl records. Mendelssohn, Beethoven and Bill Hayley made room for Guy Mitchell and others who brought us such snappy titles as *I met the cutest little eyeful (at the Eiffel Tower)* and *Does your chewing gum lose its flavour on the bedpost overnight?*

Television came to No. 47 rather later than to most homes in Newbourne. But what you don't have, you don't miss. When we weren't making our own amusement, the wireless kept us all both entertained and informed. As very young children, *Dick Barton, special agent* was regarded as unsuitable, so we listened to *Children's Hour*, with Larry the Lamb. Our parents had *Take it from here* and *Mrs Dale's Diary*. *The Archers* replaced *Dick Barton* in 1951, but it was *Educating Archie*, *The adventures of PC 49* and *Journey into space* that nourished our early-teenage imaginations much more than everyday stories of country folk. We would sit glued to a crackling radio for hours, transported to the moon or the red planet with Captain Jet Morgan, Doc, Mitch and Lemmy.

Imaginations were stretched to the limit with the *Goon Show*. Mooring a full-size cardboard model of England in the North Sea, and pulling out the plug when Hitler invaded, was much more fun to visualise on radio than it would ever have been on screen. When some episodes were later adapted for television, I refused to watch, fearful that it would destroy my perception of Henry and Minnie Crun, or Bluebottle, the squeaky-voiced boy scout from East Finchley. As the show's cheerful but gormless Eccles said, *"it was good to be alive in 1955"*.

Before the early 1950s, we didn't travel much beyond Ipswich.

Occasionally we would hire a car to visit grandparents and aunts in Essex; once or twice we travelled there by train. Apart from that, and a Sunday School outing to Lowestoft, anything not on the 232 Waldringfield to Ipswich bus route or within cycling distance was off our radar. One- or two-week family holidays were out of the question.

Then my father bought our first car, a Flying Standard 12, from Walter Tye in Hemley. How proud he must have been the first time he drove us all down the A12 to Shenfield and Brentwood. What excitement in the back on the dual carriageway around Marks Tey when the speedo hit 50 mph. Never mind the cold air from the holes in the floor – we'd soon be able to get out on the Colchester bypass and stamp our feet.

But such trips were few and far between, and not only for us. Most smallholders, even if they had a car or could afford train or coach fares, would be unable to leave their smallholdings in the spring or summer. Produce needed picking, livestock needed feeding, and family had to join casual labour to make it happen. The Chesher family home, according to Ivy Griffiths, was often full of visitors, with friends and family from other parts of the country staying with them in the summer. *"They'd spend the whole time walking,"* said Ivy, *"and would go home bronzed."* Alf Chesher, she said, had one week's holiday each year, which he spent watching horse racing in Manchester, staying with his sisters. Some joined the cricket club at Waldringfield, and others like Wally Hammond and Ernie Frost played regularly with the Woodbridge Excelsior Band.

Sheltered from the prevailing westerlies, the sandy beach at neighbouring Waldringfield was always an attraction for Newbourne children. On the banks of the River Deben, the village had been a popular sailing centre since the 1920s. The waterfront was was inaccessible to the public during the war, but once hostilities ceased, boats soon returned

Waldringfield, about 1955

85

to the river and children to the shore. Most parents were tied to their holdings, but older children could roam free, with many heading to the water by bike or on foot. George Turner, whose wife, Grace, used to keep a guest house, *Deben House*, in Cliff Road, hired out rowing boats. Ivy remembers being charged 4d an hour, and that *"some of the hours were quite long"*. She also mentions George Stephenson, from 33 Jackson Road, drowning while swimming from the beach. Accounts vary as to exactly what happened, but Mike Nunn, whose father owned the boatyard, clearly remembers rowing nearby. He was only 11 years old, and had his dinghy commandeered by those retrieving his body. Ivy says they were a much more safety-conscious after that.

We first visited Waldringfield in summer 1949, when friends of the family rented a beach hut called *Bowships* at the foot of the steps down the cliff from the car park. They stayed for a week, during which my father borrowed a boat to sail, my mother painted a picture, and we played in the sand.

Very soon afterwards, a decision was made that was to have far-reaching consequences for all of us.

13 – WALDRINGFIELD

For us children, that week by the river was a treat. It was fun for our parents, too. But it was more than that. It was a taste of something they had hankered after for years. Intangible, hard for them to put into words, but they recognised it easily enough. They had looked over the horizon beyond chickens, tomatoes and glasshouses, and liked what they saw.

Autumn came, and my father was chatting to someone on the LSA Newbourne staff. Mr Green had a beach hut at Waldringfield in what later became known as the Arab Quarter. Learning that next door to this hut was a vacant plot, my father wasted no time. Over the winter, with the help of Harry Cracknell, he built a twelve-foot by eight-foot beach hut in sections in our piggery. During spring or early summer 1950, the whole structure was taken to Waldringfield, assembled, clad in sheet aluminium, and occupied by five very excited Belchams.

Jeremy and the "biscuit tin", 1950

The hut was fondly known as the *"biscuit tin",* and is still there – just! Along with the river, beach, sailing club and, later, the Maybush Inn, it was soon playing an essential part in our lives at weekends and throughout the school summer holidays. It continued to do so until the early 1960s, when we three brothers had left home, and our parents sold it to fund a touring caravan.

Before we had a car, we had to cycle to and from Newbourne. The logistics of our first visit each year were complicated and exhausting. As we cycled through the village with bags of tins, linen, clothes and toys dangling from our handlebars, we must have raised the odd smile. I can still picture my mother pushing her bike up Samples' Hill with a meat safe balanced precariously on the handlebars.

Every year we spent all six weeks of the school summer holiday at Waldringfield. Sometimes the five of us would sleep in the hut, but

most weekdays my father had to work on the holding, and slept at home. In his twenties, he had learned to sail on the Broads, and soon found a fellow hut-owner to share ownership of a small sailing dinghy. He always tried to keep Saturdays free for sailing, but once he had taught us boys to sail and then to race, he retired to the clubhouse, and helped with race administration. The ladies in the galley, preparing teas for hungry sailors, always welcomed the misshapen – and thus unsaleable – tomatoes and eggs he brought from Newbourne. My mother, if not in the galley, would happily chat for hours on the clubhouse veranda with other mums watching their offspring afloat.

We took to it all like ducks to water. Families picknicked together and looked out for one another. Children played, swam, built dens, learned to sail and row, and got covered in mud. Teenagers raced dinghies, fell in and out of love, learned to dance to Victor Sylvester, drank cider and shandy in the Maybush, and learned to ride with Jasmine and Nettie Allen at Whitehall Farm. Friendships were made that endure to this day.

Newbourne and Waldringfield share a parish boundary. Walking between the village centres is only a gentle stroll. Families in one village have relatives in the other. But this community of beach hut and caravan owners, centred on sailing club, pub and river, seemed to have little connection with either. In spite of its seasonal nature, close bonds were formed as lives, activities and interests were shared. Out of season, sailing club dances, suppers, lectures and parties helped keep the social pot boiling. So did dinner parties, with their obligatory prawn cocktails and bottle of Blue Nun.

Work on an LSA smallholding was hands-on. It was sweaty and dirty, the hours long and unpredictable, and income depended on factors over which you had little control. You didn't own your house or your land, and your bosses were elsewhere. Outside interests meant those that lay immediately outside your back door. And most of your neighbours were in the same boat.

Small wonder then that others began to see us – when they saw us, which wasn't often – almost as outsiders. Our father was chairman of the estate's Consultative Committee, and our mother was in the WI, and delivered the parish magazine – or *"perishing magazine"*, as she sometimes called it. But for large chunks of the year, our neighbours were doctors and consultants, teachers and headteachers, insurance professionals and managing directors. Most of our playmates and friends were privately educated.

Our parents didn't always find it easy to keep up. Without a yacht, they were unable to return invitations to drinks parties on board. Booking tickets for the club's regular dinner-dances – black tie, of course – required careful budgeting. And a round of whiskeys and G&Ts at the Maybush could seriously damage their wealth.

But they persisted, not primarily for their own benefit but for that of their three sons. When income from the smallholding fell one year, our father went on the road selling some of the early felt tip pens.

Our parents gave us so much. I am always amazed and very grateful when I remember my father's willingness, when only in his mid-forties, to virtually to give up sailing for good for my benefit. He loved sailing, but sold his own boat so that I could have one to race and call my own. As for our mother, none of us ever knew how she managed to provide meals and clean clothes for us for six weeks each summer, based in less than 100 square feet of beach hut without electricity or running water, and cooking everything on a Primus stove.

Whatever she did, our mother gave it her all. She not only worked hard at Waldringfield to give us wonderful holidays, she worked like a Trojan at home and, when extra labour was needed, on the smallholding. In spite of a congenital heart defect, and a deformed spine, I never heard her grumble.

But she had been brought up in London and Brentwood. She had attended one of the few grammar schools available in the late 1920s, where she had done well. Her school reports highlighted her ability in art, English and needlework (and, to the surprise of no-one who knew her, warned that *"talkativeness"* was a hindrance!). Before marriage, she had been employed in a city office. She made clothes, loved to dress up, took care with her appearance, created an attractive garden, painted pictures, and enjoyed drama and music. She loved the woods, streams and meadows surrounding our home, and helped us appreciate them, too.

She also wrote poetry. The following, probably written after many years on the smallholding, may make us smile. But it tells us a lot about its author, and why Waldringfield and all that it involved was embraced with such enthusiasm.

THE RELUCTANT PEASANT

I'm so tired of the wind on the heath, brother!
I hate the things it does to my hair!
And I don't give a hoot
For that well-cut tweed suit!
I'd like something slinky to wear!

I'm so bored with the salt-of-the earth, brother!
Good chaps, maybe – I don't care!
I want smooth men in suits,
Not with mud on their boots!
Chanel No.5 – not fresh air!

I've had my fill of the peace and quiet, brother!
I need city lights at sun-down.
Traffic noise thrills me,
So what if it kills me!
I want to go back to the town.

I've lived too many years in the sticks, brother!
It was nice while it lasted – but please –
I want to revoke
And go back to the smoke,
And be blowed to the birds and the bees!!

© Dorrie Belcham

14 - OFF TO SCHOOL

It was September 1945 and my first day at primary school. Anthony Marks and I were perched side by side on the desk's bench seat, unable to reach the floor with our feet. Our pristine grey exercise books, inscribed *East Suffolk Education Committee*, had been proudly stored under the two sloping lids. Freshly-sharpened pencils lay in the groove at the top of the desk. The as yet empty inkwells were secure in holes beside them. Along with the rest of Standard One, we awaited instructions.

Throughout the war, most of Newbourne's infant children had been taught in the community hut behind Newbourne Hall. When peace returned, they were taught again at Waldringfield School, nearly three miles from our home in Jackson Road. But for our parents, sending us to Bucklesham School, less than a mile away as the crow flies, seemed more sensible.

To begin with, my father took me there on a saddle fixed to the crossbar of his bike – up Mill Hill, past Catts' Corner (Arthur Catt farmed at nearby Kembroke Hall early last century), and along Chapel Road. Later, he bought a pony and trap, and I was taken to school with our pony, Peggy, harnessed to a large box cart used for carrying tomatoes.

When Michael was old enough for school, he and I were allowed to walk, together with Diana and Christopher Cracknell. Later companions included Roger Salter from No. 43 and Anthony Pridham and David Newbold from No. 40. With only about 100 yards on a public road, we rarely met a soul as we scrambled and rambled across the meadows and streams, and through Bater's farm at Bucklesham Hall. Dire parental warnings meant we generally steered clear of Harry and John Bater's discarded tractors, trailers, harrows and ploughs, all enmeshed in long grass, brambles and sheep's parsley on the edge of the farm. The Bater brothers much preferred horses to machinery.

There was so much to fascinate small children. Sometimes we only heard the school bell from a distance, delayed en route by tadpoles, birds' nests or climbable trees. Scampering down Bucklesham Hall drive, and between the two hexagonal yellow painted wooden lodges we knew as the Mustard Pots, we would be just in time to join the orderly line of other pupils who probably had far less interesting journeys to school.

On our route to school, about 1945 (Pearl Simper)

Miss Cain was our headmistress. She lived in the house adjoining the Bucklesham end of the school. Miss Cain, and Mrs Lewis from Kirton, taught most of the 50 or so pupils in the schoolroom. Older children were in the smaller adjacent classroom. A large coal fire kept us warm, especially those at the front of the class. Rows of small bottles of milk were warmed on the wooden fender during the first half of each morning, and consumed eagerly at break time. Lunches were cooked by Miss Birch and Mrs Leek in the small, detached kitchen but were eaten in the schoolroom. We queued impatiently for their minced meat pie, cooked in large aluminium trays, and the dollops of swede and mashed potato. The Belchams always seemed to be at the front of the queue for seconds. Semolina was endured but pink blancmange was a treat.

The main playground was half tarmac and half grass. The grassed portion, nearest the Felixstowe Road, had a huge oak tree in the corner. Another tarmac playground, behind the schoolroom, was reserved for the girls and also used for organised games like *The farmer's in his den*, tag and *British bulldog*. Many children wore boots with studs that frequently worked loose and littered the playground. The two playgrounds were separated by a wall, against which the girls performed handstands before an appreciative audience of boys gawping through the gate.

Sanitation was basic. The two chemical toilets plus urinal for the boys were not in the same building as the washroom, so hands were rarely washed. Boys competed to see who could pee highest up the urinal's low sloping roof. Our parents encouraged us to aim high in life, but this was not what they had in mind. Boys guilty of bad language, including Michael on one occasion, were taken to the washroom to have their mouths washed out with carbolic soap. Miss Cain lived up to her name when Michael was caned in front of the whole school, and I was caned in the playground. Neither of us can remember why.

Most Newbourne children under 11 were at school in Waldringfield, and had a longer journey than we did, much of it on footpaths. *"We walked to school over fields in rain or snow, with holes in our boots,"* says John Hedley. *"We had no Wellingtons or waterproofs, and Miss Stebbings, the headmistress, wanted to know why we were late!"* Many cycled, but Georgie Madgwick, who contracted polio when very young, managed to walk the route of nearly two miles with one leg in splints. Children in Jackson Road, like Lindy and Barry Gilder, had even further to travel. Sometime after the war, transport was provided. At one stage, pupils had to squeeze into a taxi from the Fox, but this was later replaced by a bus.

Like Bucklesham School in the 1940s, Waldringfield had just two classrooms and two teachers. There was no central heating; just one open fire in the smaller room, and a big stove in the larger. It was originally the job of the bigger boys to fetch the wood and coal. The stove was also used to dry wet clothing. When it broke down, pupils had to decamp to the village hall to keep warm. A new stove was installed in 1953 after the old one burst. Barbara Kaznica (née Turner) says that *"we sometimes kept our gloves on to keep our hands warm when doing our lessons"*. She added that *"the toilets were outside in the cold, and were old buckets that had to be emptied. I was fortunate that I went home to dinner, so I rarely had to use them."* One former pupil says the boys used to wait until the girls went to the toilet, then opened the small hatch at the back and poked stinging nettles through the hole.

"At first there were no school dinners," says Barbara, who still lives in Waldringfield. *"The children who came from Hemley and Newbourne brought sandwiches and then every child had free milk to drink. When school dinners were introduced, we went over to the village hall for them, as we needed the room.*

"We had a cook and assistant, and us girls used to have to take turns helping with the vegetables and laying up the tables. The meals on the whole were very good. The only things I didn't like were lumpy custard and cabbage and the odd caterpillar." The school log noted, in September 1941, that the children had collected 89lbs of fruit on an organised school blackberrying day for the war effort.

When pupils were eleven, most transferred to the secondary modern school in Kesgrave. These included Nelson Locke, living at 35 Jackson Road in Newbourne. Nelson studied hard, and gained a university place to study agriculture. He later studied medicine, aiming to become a neurosurgeon, and achieved houseman status shortly before his tragic death from cancer in 1961.

Those who passed the 11-plus, including Lindy Gilder, Val Hill, David Thompson, Gillian Hart and David Hammond, went to Felixstowe Grammar School. Some, like John Somerville, my two brothers and myself, went to the independent Ipswich School. Others, including Sue Whittaker and the Somerville girls, chose Roman Catholic schools in Ipswich. David Dow and his brother boarded at the independent Dauntsey's School in Wiltshire.

Martlesham Heath aerodrome, July 1946

There were no buses to Kesgrave, so the council provided each pupil with a new bicycle – a white one, according to Richard Vickerstaff – a cape and leggings. But cycling across Martlesham Heath aerodrome was prohibited during the war, so Waldringfield School then had to accommodate older children as well. When 23 evacuee children were added to the mix, two classes for infants were started in the community hut at Newbourne. Barbara remembers that Miss Stebbings, *"had to go to Newbourne on certain days to supervise. That meant the infant teacher had to take charge of the head's class, and I had to teach the infants. I was about 13 at the time and thought it was great."*

The community hut stood on small, brick piles, says John Hedley, who remembers pupils crawling around underneath. *"We would have concerts, too. Ten of us boys had our faces blacked up. Someone held up a white sheet, and we sang* Ten little n***** boys."

In 1951, Mrs Benjafield from Newbourne became headmistress. Stella James (née Jones), who taught at the school, remembers that *"she took the top class and was always prim and proper despite the Lincolnshire accent. She dressed in copies of Chanel suits and had her hair done every six weeks."*

Apparently, there was nothing Mrs Benjafield disliked more than sport. The Parish Council minutes once noted: *"A complaint was made about the lack of school sports. They had been lacking for several years. Their reintroduction was strongly opposed by the Head Teacher, and she suggested that 'if the village wanted sports they could organise them'."*

Space on the playground used to be restricted by two air raid shelters, making it rather small for team games. Although these were eventually demolished, Waldringfield teams were so used to practising on a small pitch that when they played away on bigger pitches they frequently used to win. Facilities improved in 1959 when a village playing field and tennis court were opened. Swimming lessons took place in the river at high tide, with the school log for July 15th 1946 noting that *"Laurie Sample* [still living in Newbourne] *gained certificate for swimming 25 yards."* Mike Nunn recalls a teacher throwing buckets of water over the playground in winter to make a skating rink for the children! Those were the days!

An extension to the school was built in about 1958. This provided additional teaching space, a kitchen, and an office-cum-staff room where, according to Stella, *"the three teachers used to smoke like chimneys."*

15 – GROWING PAINS

Towards the end of 1949, our parents consulted Miss Cain, Bucklesham School's head mistress. They were told that, perhaps unsurprisingly in an agricultural community, educational aspirations locally were not high. If we boys were to be sure of passing our 11-plus, finding another school would be wise.

It was time for another life-changing decision. In April 1950, aged nine, I found myself at Felixstowe Academy getting to grips with French and Latin. This private school was then based in *Trevose*, formerly a doctor's house on the corner of Cobbold Road and Constable Road in Felixstowe. That summer it was moved to a large property, *Old Felixstowe House*, on Marsh Lane overlooking Kingsfleet marshes. My brother Michael joined the school in 1951. We cycled each day to Kirton, where we left our bikes at the forge and caught the bus to Felixstowe.

In addition to learning the words of *O come, all ye faithful* in Latin, we absorbed enough to get us through the 11-plus and be awarded an East Suffolk County Council scholarship – and a free bus pass – to Ipswich School. Jeremy joined the Ipswich School Preparatory Department at about the same time.

I started travelling to Ipswich in September 1951. Two years later, all three of us were trudging up Sandy Lane each morning to catch the 232 Eastern Counties bus. At various times, our fellow passengers included Rupert and Peter Bear, Jeremy Goddard, and John and Alfred Waller from Waldringfield, and Mary, Charlotte and Pauline Somerville and Sue Whittaker from Newbourne. The army cadet uniforms and boaters we sometimes had to wear caused much amusement for others on the bus.

Negotiating Sandy Lane on dark winter evenings was not easy, particularly in wet weather. We knew the location and size of each puddle, and how many paces were needed between them. But, as the bus's bright lights disappeared down Ipswich Road, we would have to wait for a moment or two to allow our eyes to adapt to the darkness. As we grew older, we preferred to cycle to school in the summer, especially once we could choose sailing instead of cricket on our three games afternoons each week. We always maintained that cycling to school each morning, then to Waldringfield in the afternoon and home in the evening, made us far fitter than the cricketers – and that was before we had done any sailing!

Under the newly-appointed headmaster, discipline was strict. Almost every aspect of life was governed by rules applying both on and off the premises. No sweets to be eaten while wearing school uniform in Ipswich. No cycling two abreast within the town boundary. No hair to be seen below the peaks of school caps, worn until the age of 16. The press had a heyday when one boy's hair was deemed too long for the school photograph. The head promptly marched him to his study and gave him a haircut. One cartoon had the miscreant afterwards complaining to his friends: *"I didn't mind the haircut, but did object to being charged sixpence."!*

Corporal punishment was administered by teachers with canes and prefects with gym shoes. Some pupils, Michael included, relished the challenge. The late Rev John Waller, Newbourne's rector, was at the school from 1952 to 1959. A fellow pupil, in an obituary for the *Old Ipswichian Journal*, wrote that John *"was a bit of a dissident, ever ready to break the rules and challenge authority – all with much amusement. He frequently received a slipper-beating from the prefects ..."* Two of us in our first year were given the same punishment for bashing one another with knotted rugby socks. Some managed to get away with smoking in the loos or with questionable activities in the showers. Others, me included, decided early on that it was wiser

Ipswich School, 1960s
(Ipswich School archives)

to toe the line. Now I sometimes wonder whether I gave too much attention to conforming to what was expected, and too little to what might have been possible. But during the decade or so following the war, creativity, individual expression and outside-the-box thinking were low on most people's lists of priorities.

However, we did receive an excellent academic education. We also learned to take some of life's hard knocks both on the sports field and in the army cadet force. There were many opportunities to develop leadership skills. The importance of public service and good manners were stressed, and were reinforced – just occasionally with a slipper – by our parents at home. On Speech Day, academic success was proclaimed and rewarded, and, best of all, our mother got to wear a large hat.

I must have been about 14 when my father, somewhat embarrassed, sat on the side of my bed and asked me whether the school was teaching me the things that boys need to know when they reach their teens. Did I need any clarification? As it happened, he was a bit too late, but I wasn't about to tell him. I was embarrassed, too, and just mumbled that all was okay.

But all was not okay. All that primary school had taught me was that *"bum"* was a naughty word. Clearly, I needed more – and fast.

My memory is that Ipswich School in those days seemed to have a two-pronged, and rather literal, approach to the birds and the bees. The bees were dealt with first in Biology. We were taught how flowers and plants reproduce, and how bees facilitate the process. The content was interesting but its relevance obscure. As for the birds, they were chickens, which were considered in great detail in Physiology. Since our baby chicks arrived pre-packed in cardboard boxes, eggs were for eating, and broody hens had to be kept in coops by themselves, this wasn't much help, either.

"pre-packed in cardboard boxes"
(LSA Charitable Trust)

Michael remembers being given a book at home, but says it did nothing to cover what all the fuss and intrigue was about. *"There simply wasn't anything about the emotional side – the why-would-some-one-want-to-do-all-that."* He felt that he would probably learn more by following couples along the river wall at Waldringfield and hiding in the grass – although *"that didn't turn out to be very conclusive either!"*

Jeremy can't recall learning anything at home or at school. Others in Newbourne were in a similar situation. *"No-one told me a thing about it,"* says Sue Whittaker. Georgie Madgwick said the same. One of my schoolmates said that he did just one year of biology, and couldn't recall anything about sex. He had been introduced to the concept when aged 10 or 11 and *"I didn't believe a word of it! What a disgusting notion!"*

For many of us it was all a bit hit and miss. No-one seemed to want to prepare us for the mental gyrations that adolescents go through. Any discussion that remotely approached the issue was, by definition, *"dirty"*, and so, as boys will be boys (particularly in an all-boys school), it became an almost mandatory topic of conversation and jokes. And of experimentation.

The result was hardly what the adults would have wanted. Sexual attraction became a world of ill-informed fantasies and unexplained instincts. I even fell in love with a girl called Elizabeth, whose photo was in most shop windows during her coronation in 1953! Dictionaries in the Northgate Street reference library allowed me to discover the meanings of words not used at home, but it was simply too daunting for a 14-year-old to ask the librarian for the books he really wanted. So, like many boys of a similar age, I continued through my teenage years always wondering why it was that everyone else seemed to know more than me.

At that age and time we had never heard the phrase *"sexual orientation"*, and were certainly never encouraged to question ours. The chickens in our school text books didn't worry about theirs, so why should we? Sometimes we wondered about others – school staff and fellow pupils – but usually only in a *"nudge-nudge, wink-wink"* kind of way.

At least those nudges and winks, however ill-informed at the time, did help me at the age of 14 to recognise something that my parents apparently had not – that a somewhat unconventional acquaintance of theirs was being rather persistent with his invitations for me to spend time alone with him. I was sufficiently aware of the danger to invent the necessary excuses.

My teenage years passed. So did most of the girls I met. One or two became girlfriends of a sort. One involved early morning assignations. I would creep out of the house at about 6 o'clock, and cycle some distance for a kiss and a cuddle – well, a cuddle anyway – in a barn.

The trouble was that I set my sights too high. Those I fell for were too good-looking not to be snatched up by boys who were bigger, richer, older or more successful than me. Some were all four. My nickname, *Half-pint*, said it all. I once went to a party in what is perhaps the poshest road in Ipswich, and fell for the girl whose birthday we were celebrating. Fat chance!

As I look back, I realise that our parents worked hard and sacrificed much to give us – with the exception perhaps of the birds and the bees – an excellent education. But we lived on the smallholding farthest from the centre of Newbourne. With most of our spare time centred on Waldringfield and the river, and our schooling in Bucklesham, Felixstowe and Ipswich, I suppose it was inevitable that we had so little involvement with village life.

16 - CHURCH OR CHAPEL?

The first prayer my mother taught me was for mice. Yes, mice. True, our cats were expected to find their own food, so any mice at No. 47 needed all the help they could get. But even at the age of four, I failed to see the need for divine intervention. Surely a daily saucer of cat food would be a simple solution?

But these mice were not at No. 47. They were somewhere called Plicity. I was mystified. But, not wishing to challenge my mother's theology, I prayed on for these unfortunate creatures. *"Gentle Jesus, meek and mild, look upon this little child. Pity mice in Plicity. Suffer me to come to Thee."*

Eventually, of course, everything became clear when I saw *"my simplicity"* in print. It was an important lesson for later life, albeit one I was slow to learn: make sure you understand what you're praying for!

Newbourne's parish church is St Mary's. A leaflet informs visitors that *"there has been a church on this site for at least 900 years with a mention of a church in Newbourne in the Domesday Book in 1086."* With its faintly damp, musty smell, it never crossed our minds as children that this was not the original building.

When the LSA arrived in 1936, the rector was Revd Percy Jamieson. I don't recall our family having much contact with either Revd Jamieson or the parish church during his time in Newbourne. Ivy Griffiths remembers him as *"very strict"*, and that he started a Sunday School when the first tenants arrived. He also established a choir that practised twice a week in the rectory, with Ernie Frost providing music on a squeezebox.

Round the corner, just before the Fox, was the Wesleyan chapel and the adjoining Chapel House. Both were built in 1868, but have been in private hands since 1973. There seemed to be more going on at the chapel, says Ivy, *"but we were 'church'"*. Ivy had attended a Church of England school in Seaham Harbour, Co Durham, before coming to Newbourne. Her family's only contact with chapel was when her sister Jean scrawled her initials, "JC", on the chapel wall – they are there to this day.

I soon learned that we were 'church'. Although my mother's family had no religious connections, my father had been confirmed and was in the choir of his family's parish church as a boy. At least two of his three unmarried sisters were Sunday School teachers. However, I have no memory of church attendance ever being part of our parents' Sundays until it was time for us to be confirmed. We were all there every Christmas, of course, nudging one other each time we sang, *"Glory to the Newbourne King"*.

But we were definitely 'church'. Some others were 'church', too. But some, who we didn't have much to do with, were 'chapel'. They seemed nice enough, but a bit distant. Or perhaps we kept them at arm's length? I was too young to know. However, in the absence of a Sunday School at St Mary's when we were old enough to benefit, most children were sent to Sunday School at the chapel. We joined them, although our attendance was best described as spasmodic. Living over a mile away, we soon discovered that, if we walked there slowly enough, we would meet the others coming out.

The difference between 'church' and 'chapel' was never explained. All we knew was that 'church' had things like altars and crosses, and services led by men in special clothes, who read prayers from books. 'Chapel' had none of those things. Chapel folk included the Buttons, Grooms and Vickerstaffs. The chapel's Sunday School superintendent was Arthur Locke, who was also a Methodist lay preacher. Arthur often preached at other local chapels and churches including Bucklesham chapel and the Baptist chapel at Waldringfield.

Ros Hart, Arthur's daughter, remembers Ernie Frost playing the organ at the chapel. *"He had rather large hands,"* she says, *"so he fumbled a bit."* Wally Hammond spoke of Ernie's organ stool collapsing during a service, and Ernie on his back on the floor roaring with laughter. Being 'church' or 'chapel' apparently didn't matter to Ernie, who was also church warden at St Mary's. Ernie's father Herbert is remembered by Ros for his long prayers, and for the noise his half-crown made when dropped on to the collection plate. Lindy Gilder taught in the chapel Sunday School in her teens, assisting a Mrs Archer, who she described as *"a lovely quiet, peaceful woman"*.

Former pupils' memories of Sunday School never seem to include the Bible stories. Brian Coates is remembered for his chewing gum, which he stuck behind his ear when told to take it out of his mouth. It inevitably became entangled with his hair, a chunk of which had to be removed by his friends after the lesson, using a piece of broken glass. Georgie Madgwick was asked to leave after letting off a jumping jack firework.

Chapel preachers often came from outside the village. These included Mr Tucker, a market gardener from Waldringfield, who arrived by pony and trap, leaving the pony tied to the horse rail outside the Fox throughout the service. Richard Vickerstaff loved carol singing round the village, *"especially at the Dows, who gave us all cakes."*

Other families, definitely regarded as 'chapel', chose to worship at Kemball Street Gospel Hall in Ipswich. These included the Baileys at 42 Jackson Road, Cyril Locke's family at 28 Mill Road and the Taylors at 29 Mill Road. The Somervilles at Newbourne Hall were Roman Catholics. So were the Whittakers at 23 Mill Road. *"We went to church in Woodbridge or Kesgrave,"* says Sue Whittaker. *"A visiting priest, Father McCormick, came to see us and stayed for Sunday tea. Once or twice I went to Sunday School in Newbourne but felt uncomfortable as I was a Catholic and didn't know many children as I went to a different school. In those days, Catholics weren't allowed to go into non-Catholic churches! Dad was Catholic but Mum was Church of England, so was in a mixed marriage."*

After Revd Jamieson resigned in 1948, Newbourne was without a rector for two years. In 1950, Revd Trevor Waller, Rector of Waldringfield and Hemley since 1948, was appointed Rector of Waldringfield and Hemley with Newbourne. Affectionately known throughout the three parishes as *"Rev Trev"*, he continued living in the rectory opposite Waldringfield church. Newbourne's rectory was bought by the Edmondsons, who sold it on to Leslie and Norah Dow in 1952.

For several years, *"Rev Trev"* undertook his pastoral visits in a Messerschmitt. This three-wheeler car was made by the company responsible for the German WW2 fighter plane, and had a similar bubble cockpit cover. The other shared feature, at least of the early models, was the absence of reverse gear. This would have been a distinct disadvantage when meeting tractors or lorries on the road to Hemley.

Trevor was often seen afloat on the River Deben in his small yacht, *Norah*, named after his wife. He always officiated at the annual Deben Week Yachtsmen's Service, accompanying the bishop upriver at the head of a flotilla of yachts, and leading the service anchored just offshore at Waldringfield. Trevor's son John followed him into the living in 1974. Both loved the river, and both were renowned and appreciated for their pastoral care, particularly of those who were sick or in hospital. Georgie Madgwick remembers *"Rev Trev"* running something called the Guild of St Edmund, and also preparing youngsters like himself for confirmation.

As a child, I am sure I was not alone in finding religion confusing. Praying for mice was bad enough. But the Bible's Adam and Eve, David and Goliath, and Noah with his arkful of animals, competed for space in our young minds with the Grimm brothers' wicked witches, Hansel and Gretel, and Rumpelstiltskin. The tooth fairy swapped any milk teeth left under our pillow for coins; Father Christmas read the letters we sent up the chimney, and filled our stockings at Christmas with all that we had asked for.

By the time I entered secondary education, I had concluded that God was very old, and lived somewhere above the clouds. He loved old buildings, old English and old people, and kept a record of all that we did. Obeying our parents and teachers, and being kind to our friends, were clearly part of keeping in his good books. So was giving up our seats to ladies on the bus, not talking with our mouths full and voting Conservative. It was vital to put our hands together and keep our eyes closed when we prayed. God much preferred prayers from a book rather than our talking with him as we did with friends. We heard about a Holy Ghost, which was a bit scary, and also about someone called Jesus, who was meek and mild, so didn't seem very exciting.

Being 'church', my brothers and I were expected to be confirmed into the Church of England. Aged 14, with many of my fellow pupils – including John Waller – I underwent confirmation preparation by the Ipswich School chaplain. It was a process involving much memorisation but minimal explanation. We had to learn by heart large parts of the 1662 Communion Service, and came across words like *"propitiation"* and *"oblation"*. In spite of not having taken part in that service for many years, with little prompting I could repeat significant chunks of it even now.

On March 14th 1955, a crocodile of boys filled the aisle of the school's small chapel, and proud parents filled the pews. We publicly assented to promises apparently made on our behalf by our godparents at our christening, after which the bishop laid hands on each pair of boys, praying that the Holy Spirit would *"ever be with them"*.

The school required us to attend chapel services twice a term, as well as an assembly with hymns and prayers at the beginning of each day. We also had religious instruction or *"Divinity"*. All were boring and totally uninspiring. Confirmation meant that we could also attend communion services, so we chose the 8.00am service at Newbourne, Hemley or Waldringfield. The rest of Sunday was then free for enjoyment.

I cannot speak for others, but for me all this was much more about conforming than confirming. It was what was expected, so it was what I did. The services I attended, the prayers I prayed, the hymns I sung, the sermons I heard – none reflected or related to what I felt inside. Confirmation had changed nothing in me. And there was no indication that it had in any of my friends. Had we missed something?

It would be another seventeen years before I realised we had. That's outside the scope of this chapter, but you can find more in *Appendix C – The penny drops*.

17 – WATER, WATER, EVERYWHERE

"*Arthur! The stream's overflowed!*" Jeanne Gilder had just pulled back the curtains. It was Sunday morning, and through the window she could see that a large part of the field opposite was under water.

A hundred yards down Jackson Road and at about the same time I looked out of my parents' bedroom window. Along the valley to the east, all I could see was a vast expanse of water between our holding and the far side of the River Deben. Jeanne was right: the stream had overflowed. So had the river.

It was February 1st 1953, and the end of a night that had seen many low lying areas of East Anglia and the Thames Estuary suffer severe flooding. Exceptional weather conditions and high spring tides, coupled with an inability to warn people, meant that whole communities were unaware of the imminent threat. Some sea and river defences were overwhelmed by the devastating storm surge and very large waves. Extensive flooding in England killed 307 people in Lincolnshire, Norfolk, Suffolk and Essex. Nineteen lost their lives in Scotland and 1800 in the Netherlands. The Meteorological Office estimated that, at today's prices, the cost of damage was about £1.2 billion.

The damage included a total of 160,000 acres of land inundated with sea water and unusable for several years. In Newbourne, 31 acres were affected, spread over 11 smallholdings on Mill Road and Jackson Road. On holdings Nos 20 and 21 practically the whole of the land up to the rear of the buildings was covered. About three-quarters of the land belonging to No. 22 was lost, as was half of that belonging to Nos 24 and 26, and about a third of that belonging to Nos 27 and 28. Smaller areas were affected at Nos 19, 36 and 38. At our home, the water just reached the edge of the holding.

The key to all this was the failure of the river wall at Kirton Creek. Salt water rushed up the valleys of the Mill River and Newbourne Stream, causing flooding of the low-lying land alongside both. David Dow remembered flooding in part of the lean-to lounge at Brook Cottage. At the water mill on Mill Road, the Mill House was flooded and the road rendered completely unusable. The army had to construct a bailey bridge until the road could be repaired.

During the Saturday night the police had learned of the approaching flood, and warned the estate manager, Ted Evans. Ted immediately organised a group to alert tenants. Wally Hammond at No. 22 remembers being woken by his neighbour Fred Jasper at No. 21. Once he'd made sure all his family were upstairs, he went outside. *"The noise of the wind was terrible,"* he said. The gale that accompanied the flooding that night is sometimes forgotten, but in Newbourne it destroyed glass worth nearly £4,000 at today's prices and damaged five huts used to house the estate's herd of pigs.

In the dark it was difficult to assess the extent of the flooding. But Wally could see that the frames in which he and Sheila had planted lettuces the previous afternoon were all under water. When daylight came, he realised they had also lost a pig hut and at least one brooder house. It was not a good start to the year – he and Sheila had only taken over the holding three months before.

Local assistance was co-ordinated by Tom Scott, the estate's pigman living at No. 23a. Georgie Madgwick and Wally both reckon that Tom's work was a major factor in getting people back on their feet, so it is sad not to find this mentioned in official correspondence. What is clear is that the LSA, locally and nationally, responded to the disaster promptly and effectively. Within two days Ted Evans had sent a preliminary report to Head Office, and included proposals for providing alternative land for the holdings worst affected. The tenants were sent a sympathetic telegram by the LSA's chairman, Sir Arthur Richmond.

On 5th February the LSA's Senior Technical Officer, Keith Wilson, visited Newbourne and assessed the losses for each holding. He found the affected tenants *"naturally despondent and somewhat bewildered"*. A report on 14th February from Ted Evans updated Keith Wilson's assessment. The major losses at that point were as follows:

> No. 19: *Some lettuce growing under cloches and a few hens.*
> No. 20: *One sow drowned; two pig houses washed away; one poultry house under water and possibly damaged; all cloches and lettuce.*
> No. 21: *Two pig huts washed away and recovered; one slatted floor poultry house under water; all cloches and lettuce.*
> No. 22: *One pig hut and two brooder houses washed away and recovered; two frames of lettuce lost.*

No. 24: One sow and approximately 50 hens drowned; two poultry houses washed away and recovered; two pig huts washed away, yet to be recovered.

No. 26: Two brooder houses washed away, one not yet recovered.

No. 27: Approximately 150 hens drowned; one poultry house blown over into the water; one poultry house washed away and recovered; two brooder houses damaged.

No. 28: No damage.

No. 36: One sow drowned; two pig houses damaged.

No. 38: No damage, but fodder beet and kale under water.

No. 47: No damage.

I sometimes wonder whether I contributed in a small way to the absence of damage at No. 28. On the Sunday morning, I helped my father load our small dinghy on to a trailer and tow it down to Mill Road. He guessed that tenants there might need help. They did, and I found myself, aged 12, proudly rowing Cyril Locke to his floating poultry house. The occupants were huddled together on perches and squawking loudly. After stuffing them into wooden crates, for which we barely had room in the boat, we were able to bring them to dry land.

Proud skipper with poultry lifeboat (in the summer!)

But there was a more important and longer-term consideration. Keith Wilson wrote, *"Of perhaps greater importance, however, is the damage to the land as the water is salt. The implications ... are serious for holdings 20 and 21 where practically the whole of the land has been flooded, and for holdings 22 and 24."* He continued, *"The lower land mainly used for livestock is still under water and possibly will remain so for an appreciable time. The upper land which has been used for cropping is likely to be out of cultivation, due to the effects of salt water, for at least twelve months."*

These issues were quickly addressed. Half the land behind the village hall was allocated to Cliff Hart from No. 20 and the other half to Fred Jasper from No. 21. Four acres on holdings 23a and 25 was split equally between Wally Hammond from No. 22 and Bill Buckles from No. 24. Each parcel of land was subject to a token rent of a shilling a year. Affected holdings were granted a reduction in rent. Some livestock, deprived of land on which to graze, was managed centrally by estate staff. Land affected by salt water was treated with gypsum, but it was three years before the worst affected land could be used again for cultivation.

From the outset, Keith Wilson and Ted Evans were concerned that the confidence of tenants on the flooded holdings would be shaken. This, they felt, was bound to colour their approach to future development and capital expenditure. By the end of February they had agreed that holdings 20, 21, 22, 24 and 26, the worst affected, should be regarded as chiefly glass and battery holdings. The limited amount of higher ground on each holding should in future be used for intensive horticulture under glass and for laying poultry kept in batteries. Each holding's battery house accommodation would therefore be increased from 200 to 400 birds. The poorer, lower land would be kept as rough grazing for rearing pullets to feed the batteries.

The importance of repairing the breach in the river wall was recognised early on. Although the high spring tides had passed, others were forecast for the end of March. Roger Salter remembers nearly all Newbourne's tenants being taken to Kirton Creek during the week following the flood to join others filling the gaps with sandbags.

Could it happen again? A fascinating and informative large-scale map at

www.suffolkcoastandheaths.org/assets/Projects--Partnerships/DEP/Deben-Estuary-Plan/FC089-10.pdf

shows the vital importance of the river wall at Kirton Creek. Provided this is maintained, Newbourne would be safe from another tidal surge similar to that of 1953. If the wall were breached, nothing could protect the estate's low-lying holdings from another disaster.

18 – HORSES AND HORSEPOWER

Horses were essential to the LSA's work in Newbourne until well after after the end of the war. As children we came across them in almost every part of the village, providing pulling power for carts, ploughs and other agricultural machinery.

In 1944, LSA Head Office circulated a memo on the care of horses. It included the following from the Journal of the Ministry of Agriculture: *"Mechanisation has loomed large in war-time agriculture, and it is unquestionable that without it our production of food would have been meagre indeed. But vital as is this mechanised arm, farm horses are still important – indeed, for certain jobs they are as indispensable today as when they were the normal form of motive power."*

Horses had been used in the village for centuries, of course. Until the end of the 1800s, theirs was the only power available for transporting people and goods and for working the land. During the inter-war years, the Suffolk Horse or Suffolk Punch was probably the working horse most widely used in Newbourne and throughout East Anglia. Dating from the sixteenth century, it is the oldest breed of heavy horse in Great Britain.

Horses in Hall Farm yard, early 1930s. Newbourne Hall is out of the picture to the right. The church is in the background. (Stan Baston)

110

Newbourne was once very well-known in horse-breeding circles. The *East Anglian Daily Times* on 24th July 1950, noted that the book *The History of the Suffolk Horse* records: *"If to the three names (Crisp, Catlin and Barthrop), which stand pre-eminent as the great names in Suffolk horses ... be added a fourth, it must be that of the late Samuel Wolton, of Newbourn Hall. In late 1853, there is little doubt that the Newbourn Hall stud was the finest in the county. No stable of mares was so well bred nor had been reared for generation after generation on the same farm in the same hands and under the same careful management. The Wolton family continued to farm Newbourn Hall under the Rowleys (the owners) until 1894."*

In 1942, Newbourne's estate manager T R Pickering received a memo from the LSA Regional Administrator. This suggested that an estate *"can satisfactorily operate with 3 horses and 3 tractors."* However, as the following correspondence shows, the process of obtaining suitable farm horses was never as straightforward as buying a tractor.

Mr Pickering told the Regional Administrator that *"The two horses I wish to dispose of are a long way past their best. One of them, in fact, broke down this spring and had to lay off for a considerable period. The very old proverb applies: 'Old horses make young men old, whereas young horses make old men young'"*

He was eventually able to replace one of the two. A farmer in Derbyshire wrote to Mr Pickering: *"Sir, I have today sent you by rail one black gelding as chosen by Mr Campbell* [possibly the LSA's Livestock Officer] *and passed by the veterinary surgeon, Mr King Clarke of Chesterfield. I think you will find the horse very serviceable and good to work in all gears. With us he has done all farm work and some trotting on road work, but he has not been left to stand unattended. I hope he will give you every satisfaction. Please find enclosed account for same. Yours faithfully, John Barber."* The price was £68, which Head Office queried because only £45 had been budgeted.

In August that year Mr Pickering complained *"the horse will not back an empty cart."* He added, *"I do like the horse in other respects, and it might be that we shall be able to teach him to back."* Nine days later he confirmed the horse was backing satisfactorily, suggesting it is *"a strange situation"* and that he is *"unaccustomed to our type of vehicle ... He is doing his work quite well."*

In early January 1943, the Head Office Livestock Officer was asked to approve the purchase of a Suffolk mare and a gelding from Mr H Kent of Hemley Hall at £100 each. The L/O replied that *"the price that is asked is probably considerably in excess of provision made in any of the estimates, but Kent's stock is so good that I should be reluctant to lose the opportunity of buying ..."*

More horses were needed in November 1943. The Regional Administrator wrote to the LSA Livestock Officer: *"The horses are required because of the increased production on the estate and the amount of additional carting being done to meet the increased number of cattle and a flock of sheep."* There is no record of these being purchased, but the great value of horses to the LSA during the war years is clear.

In March 1944, one vet reported *"The examination of the faeces taken from the Suffolk gelding revealed a very high parasitic infestation, there being 405,000 worm eggs per ounce. This is sufficient to account for the horse's poor condition and I would advise that he be treated immediately."* I wonder how long it took to count them.

Increasing mechanisation led to horsemen having to acquire new skills. Fred Pettitt and his son Bill, who had both worked almost exclusively with horses, had to learn to drive the lorries and tractors that collected produce from around the estate. Barry Gilder says that a very nasty accident was only narrowly avoided the first time Fred was put in charge of a tractor. The tractor was heading straight for the estate office, when Fred called out *"Whoaaah!"* instead of applying the brakes. Albert Baxter, who lived in Kirton, also worked for a while with the Newbourne horses, but had to stop after being injured when some horses shied. For a long while, the LSA's horses were kept in the field opposite No. 44 Jackson Road.

Others who dealt in horses of a different kind were the Bater brothers, Harry and John (Jack). They farmed at Bucklesham Hall farm from 1934 using both cart horses and tractors, but used to breed thoroughbreds. Harry's daughter, Pearl, married author and yachtsman Robert Simper, says that the brothers *"were both very keen on horses, having bred the Canadian Derby winner while farming in Canada. They used to breed thoroughbred horses at Bucklesham Hall and often sold the foals as yearlings at the Tattersall's Sale Yard at Newmarket"*.

According to census records, Newbourne had its own blacksmith at various times throughout the 19th Century. There was certainly a blacksmith's shop in Fenn Lane in 1911. But the village was without a blacksmith when the LSA arrived in 1936, so tenants had to choose between Jacobs' forge in Kirton and those in Brightwell and Martlesham, both run by a Mr Finch. Pearl Simper says that the blacksmith used by her family was Mr Finch in Brightwell. Early on he and his son also had a smithy at the bottom of the Nacton road in Bucklesham. Pearl says that they used to mend harrows and

Mare and foal at Bucklesham Hall
(Pearl Simper)

other farm machinery as well as shoe the horses.

With the arrival of the LSA, the blacksmiths must all have seen a welcome increase in business. Today, Alec Jacobs runs the Kirton forge with his younger brother Winston (so-named on account of a shared birthday with Winston Churchill). Their father was Edward, who as *"fireman"* made the horseshoes. Alec was the *"doorman"*, who removed the old shoes and fitted the new. Standing at a safe distance, we loved to watch the red hot metal being taken from the glowing furnace and fashioned on the anvil. After the seven nail-holes had been punched, the shoe would be passed to Alec. With the horse's leg between his knees, Alec would deftly apply it to the hoof amid clouds of acrid smoke. The horses seemed totally unfazed as he hammered home the nails, which always amazed us.

Other than standing too close behind one and getting kicked, my only other childhood contact with horses – or ponies, to be strictly accurate – was when my father bought a pony and trap soon after the war. What excitement we had! We were shown how to use a curry comb and the hard-bristled brush to keep Peggy looking her best. Best of all, we were sometimes allowed to sit next to our father and hold the reins. Peggy provided us with transport of a sort, but I don't think she stayed with us long. Alec Jacobs still remembers her as a bit of a handful! And she wasn't the only one. Alf Chesher had a pony and trap, too. *"Toby was reluctant to go anywhere,"* says Ivy Griffiths, *"but he could have won the Derby heading home!"*

As teenagers, Michael and I befriended Jasmine and Nettie Allen, who lived at

Peggy with author and Michael

Whitehall Farm in Waldringfield. There we learned to ride, and spent long hours exploring the fields and tracks for miles around. Tack was cleaned, horses were groomed and stables mucked out. But the pull of

Jeremy loved horses, too

the nearby river was too strong, and sailing eventually took over our lives.

In spite of the hard work of Newbourne's heavy horses, progress towards full mechanisation was irresistible. Slowly but surely these beautiful animals had to make way for another kind of horsepower. But no-one who has watched a ploughman and a pair of Suffolks cutting a straight furrow across a field of stubble, followed by a flock of white gulls, will ever forget them.

114

19 – NEWBOURNE IN LONG TROUSERS

Remembering Newbourne's heavy horses seems a good note on which to finish. They will certainly never be forgotten. But life has moved on. The men who cared for them in the early 1930s would not have recognised their village as we knew it under the Land Settlement Association. And we in turn could not have imagined Newbourne as it is today.

Much of this book harks back fondly to a previous era. It does not gloss over the unremitting hard work, war, ice-bound winters, unpredictable market prices and lack of labour-saving appliances. But it is words like *"idyllic"*, *"neighbourliness"*, *"freedom"* and *"fun"* that best describe the life remembered by most.

For Sue Whittaker, *"it was a perfect childhood."* Lindy Gilder *"had the most wonderful childhood. We didn't have much; we were poor but we were safe. I look back and think how lucky we were."* John Hedley remembers that *"we were free as birds . . . ."*

Perhaps we could define nostalgia as *"Life in short trousers relived in long trousers"*. And there's plenty of it about, at least when you get to my age! Peter De Vries' lament that *"nostalgia isn't what it used to be"* is just not true. Sometimes I have to be reminded that reliving the past is not always appreciated by those for whom it was never their present.

In his book, *The Fault in our Stars*, 2012, John Green makes an interesting statement: *"Nostalgia is a side effect of dying."* The closer we all get to our inevitable departure from this life, the more of it there is to remember and the less there is to anticipate. Looking forward reminds us of our mortality. So we prefer to look back.

To me, that's the danger of nostalgia. I can treat it as little more than a comfort blanket for the present. However, as my chapter *Church or chapel?* reminded me, beyond my mortality – three-score-years-and-ten-plus-a-bit-more-if-all-goes-well – lies immortality. That lasts considerably longer. This is probably not the place to pursue that thought, but Appendix C is a very personal sequel to *Church or chapel*. It's title, *The penny drops,* says it all.

As I said in my Preface, writing a book recalling an earlier Newbourne has been immensely interesting and enjoyable. I hope it has been equally so for those who read it. Many interesting people have told me their stories. Others are now just names from the distant past. Along with Sue, Lindy, John and others – including my brothers – I am immensely grateful for the Newbourne childhood I was given. I've also appreciated finding out more about the parents I took so much for granted.

So much has changed in the village over the past 80 years. I had to smile during a recent visit to our former home in Jackson Road, where I learned that Peter and Sue Waller, its present occupants, breed and show Newfoundlands. How appropriate, I thought, that these very large dogs should inhabit this very large house. The first tenant when it was a very small house was Jack Russell.

APPENDICES

APPENDIX A – HOLDINGS: EARLY OCCUPANCIES

HLDG	FIRST OCCUPANCY	AT DEC 1938	AT DEC 1942
1	Humphrey *Oct '37*	Humphrey	Hills
2	Woodward *Oct '37*	Hedley AE	Hedley
3	Longworth *Oct '37*	Longworth	Perrie
4	Smith A D *Oct '37*	Smith	Wilder
5	Hedley A E *Summer '37*	Mitchinson	Mitchinson
6	Young J *Oct '37*	Hedley WA	Button
7	Harrison *Summer '37*		Coates
8	Jarrett *Summer '37*	Jarrett	Ball
9	Roberts *Summer '37*	Roberts	Roberts
10	Jackson *Summer '37*	Jackson	Parsonage
11	Vickerstaff *Summer '37*	Vickerstaff	Vickerstaff
12	Iceton *Summer '37*	Iceton	Iceton
13	Johnston J *Summer '37*	Johnston	Johnston
14	Turner *Summer '37*	Lamb	Lamb
15	Proudfoot *Summer '37*	Proudfoot	Chapman
16	Gratton *30/06/37*	Gratton	Wiseman
17	Robinson *Oct '37*	Robinson	Ellis
17A	Chesher *Oct '37*	Chesher	Chesher
18	Narey *Summer '37*	Narey	Smithson
19	Mullen *Summer '37*	Webb	Madgwick
20	Price *Summer '37*		Bradley
21	Stephenson *Summer '37*		Murray
22	Webb *Summer '37*		Cheney
23	Escritt *Oct '37*	Escritt	Escritt
23a			Foster
24	Iceton A *Summer '37*		Gould
25	Angus D *late '37*		Thompson
25a	Lammond *Oct '37*		Jenkinson

26	Day *Summer '37*		Ford
27	Johnson T C *Summer '37*	Ellis	Playford
28	Raine *Summer '37*	Watling	Watling
29	Horseman *Oct '37*	Horseman	Horseman
30	Hedley W A *08/12/37*	Raine	Raine
31	Dayson *03/08/38*	Dayson	Thomas
32	Greenhalgh *24/11/37*	Greenhalgh	Kaine
33	Stephenson *late '37*	Stephenson	Stephenson
34		Warren	Abbott
35			Locke
36			Dixon
37			War Dept?
38			Cannon
39			Henderson
40			Cracknell
41			Ross-Smith
42			Doughty
43	Warren *03/08/38*	Warren	Buckler
44			Browse
45			Pettitt
46			Friend
47		Smith H W	Belcham
48		Morrow	Pickering
49		Lammond	Spurgeon
50	Smithson?		Dann
51	Perrie?		
52	Sample	Sample	Sample

Compiled from documents in Collection HC443, 'Land Settlement Association, Newbourne Estate', held on deposit at Suffolk Record Office, Ipswich Branch. Dates are for first occupancy. Tenancies would have been granted later, once training had been completed (see Chapter 4, 5th paragraph). While much care has been taken in producing this table, no assurances can be given regarding accuracy.

APPENDIX B -
DISASTER AVERTED BY BRAVE PILOT

The nine parachutists who baled out over Newbourne on November 5th 1943 (see chapter 9) were the crew of the USAAF Flying Fortress 42-3532, nicknamed the "Lucille Ball". It was based at Polebrook, Northants, south-east of Peterborough, with 511 Squadron of the 351st Bombardment Group.

The "Lucille Ball" was on only its fourth mission, and was one of 21 aircraft that set out earlier that day to bomb a synthetic oil plant in Gelsenkirchen in Germany. With its task completed, the plane was heading for home. But three of its four engines had been damaged by flak, and all three ceased working as they approached the English coast. The pilot, 2nd Lt Donald A Gaylord, brought the plane down to 3,000 feet. Soon after 3.00pm, when – according to at least one report – the fourth engine failed, he ordered his men to bale out.

He then set his autopilot on a course that would take the plane out over the sea. However, as he neared Ipswich and before he could bale out himself, he realised that the autopilot was unable to keep the plane in level flight. As it started to dive straight for a large factory, Gaylord acted quickly. Noticing an airfield nearby, he managed to pull the bomber out of its dive at 200 feet. He avoided the factory, but with no time to radio the control tower or to lower the undercarriage, crash-landed at Ipswich Airfield. The bomber was later repaired and flown back to Polebrook, but there is no record of any further missions. In spring 1944 a new Fortress was named the "Lucille Ball II" by James Cagney on behalf of the actress.

I wonder whether the factory workers –

BOMBER PILOT GAYLORD WINS HERO'S PRAISE

Former Waterloo Youth Is Credited with Saving Fortress, Crew.

Lt. Donald A. Gaylord, 23-year-old Waterloo bomber pilot, yesterday was credited in a press dispatch from southern England with risking his own life to save his fellow-crewmen aboard a battle-scarred Flying Fortress after a mission over Germany on Nov. 5.

Lieutenant Gaylord, son of Mr. and Mrs. A. S. Gaylord, now in Richmond, Cal., and husband of Mrs. Verona Gaylord, now residing here, reportedly brought his stricken Fortress —"Lucille Ball" — home on one engine after a raid over Gelsenkirchen.

A press dis-
patch received here said it was the Waterloo youth's second mission over Europe.

West Graduate in '37.

Lieutenant Gaylord was a 1937 graduate of West high school, and earned his commission at Luke Field, Ariz., in April this year.

Describing the heroism shown by the pilot, the Associated Press reported the Fortress almost crashed when over the city of Ipswitch, in England, after other members of the crew had abandoned the plane, leaving Gaylord at the controls.

Limping home from the big raid, the Fortress had its horizontal stabilizer shot off and its nose smashed by a propeller that flew off a shattered engine.

Finally it was down to one working engine when it reached the British coast.

It Goes Into Dive.

Gaylord ordered the crew to bail out, pointed the ship toward the sea, set the automatic pilot and was just preparing to jump out himself when the damaged controls put the plane in a steep dive.

Gaylord scrambled back to the pilot's cabin, pulled the plane level 200 feet above the buildings of Ipswich, and succeeded in making a crash landing in a field outside the city.

Other members of the crew included Sgt. Clarence A. Rowlinson, Le Grand, Ia.

All members of the crew returned to their base safely.

120

presumably at Cranes – ever learned how a pilot's courage kept them from otherwise certain disaster.

2nd Lt Gaylord was unscathed and continued flying until the war ended. When he retired in 1975, he was a Brigadier General, and commander, Pacific Exchange System, Honolulu, Hawaii. He was responsible for an overseas area exceeding 12 million square miles of the worldwide Army and Air Force Exchange Service.

The crew that day were:

2nd Lt Donald A Gaylord, Pilot (born 1920, died 1998); 2nd Lt Howard G Smith, Co-pilot; 2nd Lt Max G Simmons, Navigator; 2nd Lt Conrad G Womble, Bombardier; S/Sgt Paul B Smith, Top Turret (born 1923, single); S/Sgt William T Palmer Jr, Radio operator (born 1920, died 2000); Sgt Robert H Rumbaugh, Left waist gunner (born 1920, married); Sgt Clarence A Rowlison, Right waist gunner (born 1922, shot down over N Sea Dec 1943); S/Sgt John Byrne, Ball turret (born 1912, single); S/Sgt Sam Walton, Tail gunner (born 1922, married).

It is sobering to see the ages of these men. Paul Smith was only 20. Clarence Rowlison was 21, and lost his life only a few weeks later when his plane was shot down over the North Sea. Sam Walton was the same age. Donald Gaylord, William Palmer and Robert Rumbaugh were 23. All could have been just out of university.

My brother Michael managed to track down the family of William T Palmer, and contacted his son Richard in Florida. Replying, Richard wrote, *"My father generally tried to keep any conversation about his time in the war light-hearted and entertaining. On a few occasions, his mood became very somber when I asked him of the trips themselves. As the radio operator, he was to have remained at his rig for the duration of the trip, even while maintaining radio silence. He mentioned that hearing the local communications among the crew and not being able to assist or fill in for injured crew mates as the most difficult thing he had ever encountered. He mentioned that it was a helpless feeling and the remembrance of it affected how he reacted to things for the rest of his life. I often felt that he suffered from PTSD, although he would have never admitted such a thing and on more than one occasion when the subject of PTSD came up, he would say, 'Anything is better than Post Traumatic Dead Disorder.' Certainly a different kind of cat from a different era."*

In a lighter vein, Richard added that, *"My father actually was forced to bale out on two separate occasions. The one in particular that I remember most was his recollection of being forced out of the plane quickly, without time to lace his boots. As his parachute popped, his boots fell off and he landed in a pig pen, cold and in stockinged feet."*

He concluded, *"On behalf of my family, thank you so much for showing an interest in our 'Daddy.'"*

Did anyone in Newbourne find his boots?

SOURCES

Felixstowe Police Report: (718) Friday, 5th November, 1943

Randy Burton, 351st Bomb Group Members' Association

Alan Smith, Museum Archivist, Martlesham Heath Aviation Society

APPENDIX C – THE PENNY DROPS

Just inside Newbourne churchyard, on the right of the path, is a large and impressive grave monument, surrounded by railings. It's rather stained and weather-beaten now, but when I was a child it always seemed to be dazzling white.

I've often thought of that monument whenever I've read in the Bible about Jesus' denunciation of the religious leaders of his day. They were, he said, like *"whitewashed tombs"* that look impressive on the outside but inside are full of dead men's bones and everything unpleasant.

Strong words. But it wasn't until 1971 that I realised they also applied to me.

I'm not sure what I had expected would happen at confirmation. But, as I wrote in the chapter, *Church or chapel?*, nothing did. I dutifully continued to attend church, but deep down I still sensed I was missing something important.

After leaving home at 18, I became increasingly religious. There was church each Sunday – sometimes twice. Cathedral, city centre church, village church, chapel – I tried them all. I sung hymns as prescribed, worked hard for the church, and attended every church function.

But God still seemed far away. I tried hard to obey him, but had no idea whether I was doing enough to earn his approval. As for a long-term future in heaven – or the other place – I had no idea. I read the Bible daily, but had no idea how much of it I could believe. I prayed each day but never saw or even expected answers. A vague sense of guilt persisted.

Occasionally, however, I met religious people who seemed different. In fact, they didn't seem to regard themselves as religious at all, probably mindful of Jesus' strong words to those religious leaders. They clearly had something I hadn't. In our sitting room late one evening in 1971, I told one of them my story and awaited his reaction.

After about twenty minutes I realised I had a choice. I could continue to wear myself out trying to please God but never knowing whether I had done enough. Or I could accept his verdict that I could never do enough, however hard I tried. However religious I was on the outside, the inside would always disqualify me from a personal relationship with him.

I didn't feel that arguing with God was a good idea. In any case, what I'd just been told was the only thing that made sense of what I'd heard, read and sung about for years. God's solution to my problem was Jesus on the cross – his death in my place – and his resurrection.

"Perhaps we should pray," said my friend. There and then we knelt by our armchairs. Filled with sudden and profound thankfulness, I acknowledged my need of forgiveness, and committed my life to God.

There were no flashing lights – just a real sense that a great load had been lifted. This was certainly not something anyone had planned, let alone orchestrated. As I stood up after a few minutes, probably with a stupid grin on my face, I was very conscious of a peace I had not known before.

In the days that followed, I noticed several very specific things. First, I knew I was forgiven. The sense of guilt had simply disappeared, to be replaced by a firm assurance that heaven awaited me when I died. I also just knew that the Bible was true from beginning to end, even though there were – and still are – several bits I could not understand. More than that, its relevance to life here and now became startlingly clear.

Worship services became a pleasure rather than a duty. And prayers were answered, sometimes in quite remarkable ways. Last, but by no means least – and this was not anything I specifically asked for or even expected – I began to experience a desire to do what pleased God, and the ability to carry it out. The inclination to satisfy my own needs and do things my way was still there – and still is – but it somehow seemed to have lost its power.

Life from then on changed radically, just as the Bible promises. However, that story would need another book!

I recognise that not everyone will want to read this. That's why it's included as an appendix. But if just one reader feels, like I did, that they are *"missing something important",* then this may be for them, and writing it will have been worthwhile.

If you are that reader, I recommend the website

www.christianityexplored.org.

For anyone preferring a paper version, the small book, *One life. What's it all about?* is free on request from the publisher – see second page for address etc.

(Matthew 23 verse 27)*

124

APPENDIX D -
THE LAND SETTLEMENT ASSOCIATION:
ITS RISE AND DEMISE

GOOD INTENTIONS

The Land Settlement Association was established in 1934 during the industrial depression. Several organisations including the Carnegie United Kingdom Trust worked with the government to devise and jointly fund a scheme to help unemployed industrial workers become self-supporting smallholders.

The idea of land settlement in Britain was initially conceived as a means of providing opportunities for returning soldiers after the First World War. However, in the 1930s it was the long-term unemployed men in the Special Areas of Durham, Northumberland, Cumberland and south Wales that were of particular concern.

Soon after the LSA was formed, the government appointed a Commissioner for the Special Areas, who invited the association to establish on his behalf approximately 1,000 smallholdings. By the outbreak of war in 1939 this target had been exceeded, with 440 tenants in place and 409 men undergoing training. A separate scheme was established for south Wales.

Those accepted as trainees were aged between 30 and 50, with wives who supported the move. The first three months of training mostly involved preparing the holdings; for some this included helping to build the houses in which they and their families would eventually live. Three months of more intensive training were followed by an assessment. Successful trainees would then be allocated a smallholding, where they would be joined by their wives and children.

For a further twelve months, and sometimes longer, the men were still classed as trainees, and could continue to draw unemployment benefit and the training supplement. They paid rent for their accommodation, but buildings and equipment on their holdings, and any marketable produce, remained the property of the LSA. Once they became tenants, they were entirely dependent on profits from their holding. Many took advantage of loans available through the LSA.

On May 8th 1939 an article in *The Times* noted that the Land Settlement Association was by then the largest producer of foodstuffs in the British Isles. The newspaper pointed out that the LSA had been developed not only during a time of industrial depression but of agricultural depression, too. Yet this unique experiment had made substantial strides and experienced significant success.

When the war began, the pool of unemployed able-bodied men quickly dried up. Some found ready employment in munitions manufacturing and other war-related occupations while many signed up for active service. Over 200 holdings were vacant. Government funding for the scheme ceased and the association began recruiting men with agricultural experience and some capital of their own. Within a year over 100 of these Agricultural Tenants had been admitted, and hardly any trainees remained.

HOW IT WORKED

It was clear from the outset that the association needed to control the production and marketing of produce, and the sourcing and supply of seeds, fertilisers and other necessities. It also needed to provide technical and other advice as required.

In addition to the London Head Office, each settlement had an Estate Service Depot (ESD) controlled by an estate manager. Each needed about 50 smallholdings to be viable, with production focusing on horticulture (fruit and vegetables), poultry and pigs.

Livestock holdings needed seven to ten acres, and horticultural holdings up to five acres. A few of the larger holdings also grew cereal crops. All had a heated glasshouse and a piggery; some had a battery house for poultry.

Each ESD collected the tenants' produce, and had a Packing Station where it was graded and prepared for the large city wholesale markets. Tenants purchased fertiliser, fuel, packaging, tools and other sundries from the Stores; tractors and other heavy machinery, operated by the ESD's Service Department, were available for hire. The Estate Office kept records of all tenants' transactions, and provided monthly and annual statements.

An estate Propagation Department (or "Prop") provided plants for all the major horticultural crops. They also tested seeds and demonstrated methods of cultivation and varieties of crops. At least three Technical Assistants were appointed on each estate. One was an expert in horticulture and responsible for the Prop. Another was expert in poultry, overseeing all breeding on the estate and controlling disease. The other was a pig expert, supervising breeding, marketing of surplus animals, castration and inoculation.

Every estate had a community hut; some had a full-time social secretary. After the war social and cultural activities grew considerably.

EARLY ASSESSMENTS

An assessment of how the scheme had worked during the war was provided in *The Field* on June 14th 1947. Correspondent Ralph Whitlock had visited Newbourne a year earlier and wrote that *"here was a community, engaged in agriculture on modern, scientific lines and producing both commercial profits and contented people. 'If this is the future,' I thought, 'it works.'"* Yet he confessed to being *"assailed with doubts."* His concern was that the war had made profits inevitable for efficient smallholders, but recent statistics had shown that the profitability of farming was rapidly falling. He also wondered about the number of administrative staff, both locally and at LSA head office in London. *"Basically,"* he said, *"these people produce nothing and therefore they are dependent on what is produced on the estates."*

When Mr Whitlock returned to Newbourne 12 years later he was *"pleased and a little surprised to find the settlement still prosperous and flourishing."* In an article, *Farming costs shared* in *The Field* in 1958, he noted that *"as for the administration, there has apparently been some wise pruning, with good results."* Estates, now numbering 18, had 821 occupied holdings. Acceptance requirements for would-be tenants had been raised to at least five years' relevant experience plus capital of between £1,500 to £2,000. However, up to 75% of the capital could be borrowed through a ministry scheme.

The article noted that *"over the five years ending in 1956, the average return to the tenants of the 821 holdings, after paying all outgoings, had been about £600 a year. In 1953 to 1954, the average earnings from as representative a group of farms of 50 acres or less as it was possible to find came to between £360 and £470."* Mr Whitlock maintained that the LSA's favourable comparison was not down to joint marketing but because *"the central estate, by providing the numerous services outlined above, relieves the tenant of the necessity of investing his limited capital in such things. That is what a true farming co-operative should do, and what most of our co-operative societies do not do."*

BEHIND THE SCENES

In 1947, while readers of *The Field* were assimilating Mr Whitlock's report of his first visit to Newbourne, the government was setting up a committee to review the LSA's operation. Chaired by George Brown (later Lord George Brown), it was required to address two important concerns: 1. The LSA had paid its way during the war years, but losses had reappeared in peacetime, with no interest yet having been paid on the government's capital loan; and 2. The LSA's relationship with its tenants needed improvement. Experienced tenants felt restricted and inadequately consulted, and received no share in any profits of the compulsory marketing service.

To understand the background – indeed, to understand the full history of the LSA and its eventual demise – it is essential to appreciate the factors determining its relationship with its tenants. Most important of these was the Tenancy Agreement, drawn up in 1936. This ensured protection of a key element of the scheme, namely its absolute control over the marketing of a tenant's produce, the purchase of his supplies, the cropping plan he followed and the advice he was given.

An obstacle to this approach was the Agricultural Holdings Act 1923. In addition to ensuring security of tenure, this upheld a tenant's right to crop his farm and market his produce without interference. The LSA eventually avoided this by using 364-day tenancies, which were not protected by the act.

The LSA Executive Committee was determined to enforce co-operative buying and marketing and acceptance of the estate manager's advice. Tenant representation in the management of estates was acceptable, but tenants could only share control of their holdings with the LSA and could have no control of marketing. The Tenancy Agreement reflected these intentions.

Peter Clarke, in his 2012 paper *The Land Settlement Association (LSA): its Co-operative Ideals and their Implementation*, says that the LSA could never give the men control of their estates. *"They could not afford to fail,"* he says. *"Too much public finding was at stake."* He concluded that *"The scheme had held out the hope of a new life with a degree of self-determination and freedom but in reality the men had to heed the LSA's advice, follow the LSA's cropping plan, take their supplies from the LSA and market their outputs exclusively via the LSA. Sales at the farm gate or at their own initiative was forbidden by the Tenancy Agreement; it was 'illicit selling' which could lead to dismissal from the scheme."*

In 1947, when it became clear that the LSA would never be able to service its capital loan from the Commissioner for the Special Areas, legislation was passed that enabled the LSA's debts to the government to be liquidated. Its assets passed into the control of the Minister of Agriculture and Fisheries (MAFF), and the LSA became an agent for the government.

From 1948, the aim of the scheme was to afford *"men with agricultural experience an opportunity to become farmers on their own account."* Agricultural labourers could progress to become farmers on a larger scale.

BROWNED OFF

Lord George Brown published his report in 1950. The compulsory marketing and purchasing schemes were sound in principle, he said, but he was concerned that margins on bulk purchasing were entirely absorbed by overheads and the cost of other services. Tenants received no direct cash advantage by using the scheme.

Lord Brown also felt that the size of the national headquarters, the over-elaborate structure of central and regional control and the consequent heavy wage bill and other administrative costs were difficult to justify. He recommended that estate managers deal direct with Head Office, that the considerable volume of paperwork be reduced, and that a tenant be put on the Executive Committee. The immediate aim, he said, was that the scheme should become self-supporting. He also urged that tenants be granted 365-day tenancies to give them security of tenure.

The outcome was the 1951 Memorandum of Agreement (later called the Blue Book) between the minister, the LSA and the National Association of LSA Tenants (NALSAT). The minister appointed two additional members to the Executive Committee selected from names

129

suggested by NALSAT. Ultimate responsibility for decisions on all matters would continue to rest with the Ministry of Agriculture as the owner of the estates. Lord Brown's recommendation that tenants be granted 365-day tenancies was accepted, and effected in October 1951. This gave tenants security of tenure and entitlement to compensation on quitting the holding. However, control over the cropping of the smallholdings and the marketing of produce was retained by means of a scheme approved by the minister under a sub-section of the 1948 Agricultural Holdings Act. Virtually all requisites still had to be purchased through the association.

Tenants were generally disappointed, feeling that little had been achieved. Some were resentful. Admittedly, they now had representatives on the Executive Committee, but these were appointed by the minister. In any case, the committee was not obliged to act on their recommendations. Complete control over cropping, marketing and purchasing was retained by the association. The only positives were a slightly more streamlined administrative structure, improved security of tenure and compensation on quitting.

CONSOLIDATION AND COMPETITION

K J McReady in 1974, in his booklet *The Land Settlement Association: Its history and present form*, says that the period from the 1950s to the mid-1960s *"marked a very important stage in the development of the LSA ... Strengths were consolidated and secure foundations laid."*

The period saw a steady move towards commercial horticulture, and success in making the Central Services self-supporting. By 1965 Central Services had generated significant surpluses, and the number of experienced growers had continued to increase significantly. The objective was now to assist tenants to build up sufficient capital to allow them progress up the farming ladder. Alongside this, the association recognised the importance of marketing rather than selling. Specialisation in horticulture was increasingly seen as the way ahead, as profiting from poultry or pigs was proving more and more difficult. Horticultural production increased steadily throughout the period.

Profitability of smallholdings during the 1950s and early 1960s was affected by two other factors, both outside the control of growers.

The first was the exceptionally severe winter of 1962/63. Fuel for heated glasshouses was being burned at an alarming rate. In what he described as his *"factually correct story of what actually happened in the village of Newbourne from October 1951 until December 1983,"* Newbourne tenant Dick Whittaker wrote, *"The frost finally relented and gave up its grip. When the first hearted lettuces were harvested they made a magnificent price, which rewarded those growers who had kept the frost out of their glasshouses."*

The second factor was increasing competition from Dutch growers. *"The Dutch dominated the English markets with produce ... for much of the early season,"* said Dick. *"Their government believed in a strong horticulture and were forever coming up with ideas to improve the lot of their growers ... multi-acre blocks of glass became common."* What he and others found particularly galling was that, while the English had to heat their glass using oil or coal, the Dutch had vast reserves of natural gas which they could obtain at subsidised rates. This was never resolved, he said, until Britain became a member of the EEC. Even then the subsidies were not removed for another three years.

WISE WORDS

In 1963 the Minister of Agriculture commissioned a report from a committee chaired by Professor M J Wise. The committee interviewed estate committees as well as individual tenants, including those in Newbourne.

The report was submitted in April 1967. It found that the concept of the LSA being the first rung on the farming ladder was no longer appropriate. Nor was it in any real sense a co-operative – *"compulsory co-operative"* was a better description. Relationships between the association and tenants still needed improvement, and dissatisfaction with centralised services remained a source of continued frustration.

It appeared to Professor Wise that the benefits of bulk purchasing were swallowed up by administrative costs and/or maintaining the London Head Office. The element of compulsion worked against efficiency in management by removing the competitive factor. Profits made on profitable estates were subsidising those in deficit; it would be better to sell unprofitable estates. Smaller items could be purchased locally at the same price and with less delay. Most estates wanted purchasing and marketing to be run at estate level.

Many established and prosperous tenants felt that central accounting services were valueless. Most had their own accountants, and objected to having to pay towards central provision. They felt the same about the Establishment Charge, which all tenants had to pay to cover the time that association officers devoted to individual tenants on matters not connected with the central services. Unsurprisingly, use of the LSA's own insurance, compulsory even for a grower's own glass, was unpopular, too.

Professor Wise concluded that there was a strong desire, particularly among the more prosperous smallholders, that the estates be turned into autonomous co-operatives. His committee felt that the scheme could serve a useful purpose by leading smallholders into voluntary co-operation, accomplished in one of two ways.

The first, Scheme A, was a modification of the present scheme. The second was Scheme B, which involved the formation of autonomous estate co-operatives. For both schemes, the committee recommended ways in which they could be implemented.

Professor Wise favoured Scheme B. A number of the successful estates were already prepared to function as independent co-operatives. There was no justification for supporting the present scheme indefinitely out of public funds, and retaining the element of compulsion that would be required under Scheme A would provoke widespread dissatisfaction.

He also believed that Scheme B would not only encourage voluntary co-operation but also organised cropping and marketing, and the maintenance of the high standards and goodwill associated with the LSA trademark. It accorded with present trends in co-operation and could serve as a model in voluntary horticultural co-operation in a way that the present scheme and Scheme A could not.

DECISION TIME

The minister received the report in April 1967 and made his statement on the future of the scheme in May 1968. The present scheme would continue but with some modification. It would concentrate on horticulture; stock-based estates would leave the scheme. The LSA Executive Committee would propose ways of increasing co-operation with tenants.

Seven estates were then closed and another closed a few years later. Ten remained. Four tenants were appointed to the Executive Committee by the LSA, and central purchasing was retained with minor modifications.

Tenants' reactions were mixed. Some would have preferred Scheme A, some Scheme B. The consensus was against forming co-operatives. But Central Purchasing and the Establishment Charge were still strongly objected to. Objections were raised by their representatives in London but to no avail. *"Serfdom was to be continued,"* said one tenant.

With the onset of the 1970s, the reverberations largely subsided. Some felt that the cracks had simply been papered over. Soon after the report was published, it was said, one third of the growers were bankrupt, one third as good as, and only a third viable.

The minister then embarked on a vast modernisation scheme, ready for entry into the Common Market. Grants of 25% for replacing old glass were made available, soon followed by grants of 40% for new glasshouses. Some tenants questioned where the new markets were. What would happen when tariffs against Dutch produce were removed? Tomatoes were now yielding 100 tons per acre, and production from the Netherlands was increasing. 1975 and 1976 were both heatwave years. But modern glass was erected at great expense, all provided with heaters in spite of the rising cost of oil.

This period saw rampant inflation, the fuel crisis and rocketing interest rates. Then, in the mid-1970s, the 40% grant was withdrawn. Servicing of capital became critical, and growers needed to work even harder just to stand still. The family unit that owned its own equipment was best placed for survival, but even that business meant long hours of unremitting toil and a great deal of managerial skill. With the price of the end product remaining static, many incoming tenants were unable to service the capital. Established growers were incensed, especially at a scheme that meant they faced extra charges to pay off the growing debt that they themselves had not incurred. Dick Whittaker felt *"it was a recipe for disaster."*

The LSA debt ran into millions and was increasing, said Dick. *"By 1978 the game was up. Interest rates were pushing 17% to 20% and the salad trade was becoming saturated. The OPEC alliance was chasing the oil dollar, and eastern bloc countries were raising vast areas of glass for salad production to seek western currencies and raise their flagging economies. This pushed the Dutch and French increasingly into the British market This was especially attractive because our high interest rates had made the pound a much sought-after currency. Spain and Greece applied for EEC membership and Albanian tomatoes appeared on the London markets."*

In 1979 the tomato market collapsed. There was vast over-production, and during that August Class 1 tomatoes were dumped. *"Dig a hole and bury them,"* was the cry, said Dick. But they still had to be picked. They were no good for soup, canners preferring the Italian outdoor tomato which was more suited to processing. Agreements to hold back fruit from markets were not always honoured by estates. Then, in the first half of 1980 the lettuce market collapsed. The cracks papered over following the Wise Report widened. Newer growers who had built their businesses on the crest of the grant-scheme wave, the availability of easy money, and a *"live now, pay later"* approach, were hardest hit. Servicing the capital expenditure of the previous five years or so was impossible. Younger growers ran into debt and older growers had to resort to their savings. *"A cloud of despondency settled over the village,"* said Dick.

JOINT REPORTS

In early 1980 tenants from the 10 estates refused to agree an increase in prices and charges for the centralised services which would be effective from April 1st. They took the minister to arbitration.

The Minister engaged PA International Management Consultants Ltd to enquire into LSA Central Services aspects (but not marketing) – their fairness and viability. They only had 2 months!

Following their own quick comparison of prices of like-for-like items included in the requisite purchases scheme, PA Consultants said that *"it appears likely that as long as the compulsory system pertains, there will continue to be disagreement between the LSA and growers over prices."* They added that there was little incentive at estate level for management to be innovative in order to make savings on the services provided.

At the same time the LSA Executive Committee engaged the Central Council for Agricultural and Horticultural Co-operation (CCAHC) to enquire into the marketing side of the association. Their

134

report would be used in conjunction with the PA Consultants' Report.

The CCAHC Report strongly favoured co-operatives controlled by the growers, and said that, if Professor Wise's Scheme B had been instigated in 1967, the study *"would have portrayed a healthier picture"*. CCAHC attempted to demonstrate that in 1977, 1978 and 1979 LSA tenant growers were disadvantaged to the tune of over £1 million as a result of inadequate production/marketing planning.

The LSA's philosophy was production-driven, said CCAHC, with little attention given to avoiding sending bulk pickings to market in a glut. Many LSA growers were production- rather than market-orientated. One large co-operative regarded the LSA as weak sellers.

CCAHC also said that the rules of the LSA did not conform to co-operative principles. Neither the Executive Committee nor Standing Committee were accountable to tenants.

From the two reports it was clear that the need was to form proper co-operatives and give increased latitude to purchasing by growers – exactly what had been recommended by Professor Wise 15 years earlier but had been turned down.

However, the LSA Executive Committee decided to leave the LSA more or less as it was, but to remove the compulsory purchase of requisites excluding packaging and fuel oil. The formation of co-operatives was rejected out of hand.

The tenants rejected the proposals and stood their ground. Estates were in touch with their MPs, and moves were made to litigate against the compulsory purchase clause if not ceded.

The minister then intervened. He promised that marketing would still be done centrally but steps would be taken to improve its effectiveness. Administrative costs would be reduced and the central purchasing department closed as soon as possible. Purchasing of most growers' requisites would be done at estate level. There would be improved representation by, and consultation with, tenants.

Tenants were cautiously welcoming. They were being given all they had been asking for years. All their MPs were supportive. But they were still very concerned that the monumental debt problem could not be resolved.

BEGINNING OF THE END

Until then, debt had been financed either by successful growers or by the ministry – in other word, the taxpayers. At March 1981, some estates were in surplus, others in deficit by many tens of thousands of pounds. But each grower was responsible, whether or not they were prudent. It was not the fault of the prudent, but they could do nothing about it.

Slimming down was attempted. Redundancies were made, services curtailed, and moves made towards co-operatives with a central marketing body. Bonuses on turnover and sales were drastically cut.

In February 1982, the ministry began to look at the LSA's long-term financial future. They indicated that forming co-operatives with a central marketing organisation was their intention, and would be working towards a higher proportion of sales into the multiple stores. There would be a greater grower involvement in running the association, and they were committed to ensuring the LSA had a long-term future. The Minister talked of setting the Central Reserve Fund against the debt. This had been built up over a quarter of a century, and in 1981 stood at a quarter of a million pounds.

The good growers, who were mostly responsible for the healthy state of the Central Reserve Fund, were most unhappy. In Newbourne, a tenants' committee was elected by secret ballot, and advice sought from their MP. On November 11th 1982, several of the committee went with the MP to London to make representation to the minister. There they raised the issue of bad debt, which stood at approximately £1.5 million, and were appalled to learn that moves were afoot for new tenants not to have any responsibility for former debt. They pointed out that efficient growers, who had incurred no debt, would still be responsible.

Other concerns were mentioned by the tenants. The minister listened intently, and promised urgent action in the very near future. But he added that the solution would not please everyone.

WINDING UP

On 1st December 1982, the Rt Hon Peter Walker MP, Minister of Agriculture, Fisheries and Food, made a statement in parliament concerning the future of the ten LSA estates. In summary, the Land Settlement Association was to close down.

On LSA estates around the country the news was greeted with

mixed feelings, and with some trepidation. In Newbourne, the news was broken with a phone call from another estate at 7.30pm.

The minister stated that tenants would become responsible for their own marketing as soon as possible, using individual estate co-operatives and other existing marketing organisations. The association's present marketing arrangements would be terminated in early April 1983. LSA facilities and equipment would be available for lease or purchase on commercial terms. Tenants would have the opportunity to buy the freehold of their own smallholdings at the tenanted valuation, but their debts would have to be cleared before any offer of purchase could be made. The minister also confirmed that tenants' representatives would be consulted in initiating these changes.

A meeting on 3rd December in Newbourne Village Hall was crowded. Most growers were in favour of running their own affairs but those in financial straits were not. Their main concern was how to fund the purchases of their freeholds and the formation of a co-operative. At a meeting of Newbourne tenants a week later, it was announced that the LSA's bad debt was £1.8 million and the outstanding debt over £7 million.

Nationally, concern was expressed that overseas competitors would be able to capitalise on the LSA's demise. In Hansard on 20th December 1982, Mr Stanley Newens, MP for Harlow, is recorded as saying that *"About 500 growers on 10 estates are involved, and the LSA is the largest producer of salad crops in Britain. If the LSA marketing arrangement is not adequately replaced, the market for those products will be taken up by somebody else. Growers in the Netherlands and other European countries would be only too glad to take advantage of such an opportunity."*

Following the minister's announcement, a valuation of each holding was carried out by LSA-appointed valuers. Figures for compensation were often disputed and property valuations challenged.

On January 19th 1983, the minister told the House of Commons that the LSA's marketing services, previously due to end on March 31st, would continue to the end of the year as "LSA '83" for those who wished to use them. The repayment period for Short-term Credits would also be extended to that date.

Many meetings were held over the next few months, at both local and national level. Disagreements sometimes resulted in bad feeling and division on estates. Dick Whittaker records that, just before

Christmas 1982, a speculator had a look round with a view to purchasing the Newbourne estate lock, stock and barrel.

OUT OF THE ASHES

On April 1st 1983 the LSA fragmented into nine or ten separate units of production based on the former estates. Two estates formed their own co-operatives, simply changing the logo on the packing materials and substituting their own brand name, and continuing to supply the same customers. Other estates set about making their own marketing arrangements or joining with existing co-operatives. Some went it alone, forming small marketing groups to service the market salesmen. They were courted by many who were keen to get a slice of about £10 million of produce, good produce at that. Others opted to stay under the umbrella of "LSA '83" until the end of the year. Some continued on their own after that date.

In Newbourne, ten former tenants formed Newbourne Growers Ltd. This became a founder production co-operative of Home Grown Salads, launched on January 1st 1984. Three other former LSA estates – Foxash in Essex, Fulney in Lincolnshire and Fen Drayton near Cambridge – were also incorporated in HGS. In spite of difficult marketing conditions, both Newbourne Growers and HGS had encouraging sales during their first year of trading.

Snaith Salad Growers Ltd in the East Riding of Yorkshire is today a growers co-operative formed in 1983 following the LSA's closure, while Bedfordshire Growers Ltd is a large horticultural co-operative with links to the LSA's former Potton estate.

Philip Hamlett, who worked with the LSA for over 40 years, was manager of several estates including Abington and Fen Drayton. After the closure, he acted as consultant for the MAAF. In October 2005, he published *The Land Settlement Association Ltd, 1934 – 1983: An epilogue.* His section, *Progress of the estates after the closure,* shows that the various marketing schemes followed by the former LSA estates met differing degrees of success. Most fragmented, he says, and some went out of business. Smallholdings were sometimes sold for use as garden centres or for stabling horses. Today in Newbourne, two beautifully landscaped former smallholdings of several acres have been put on show to the public during Open Gardens events. But some glasshouses, structures and piggeries are derelict and overgrown.

Those who recall the general tidiness and neighbourliness of the LSA estates miss the old days.

LITIGATION

Following the LSA's closure, about half the tenants, including 60 from the Newbourne and Foxash estates, took the minister to court. They alleged that his unilateral action was a breach of contract and claimed compensation for expenses arising from setting up their private businesses. The 292 litigants were represented by a team of 19 solicitors and six barristers in the High Court proceedings. Ipswich solicitor Richard Hemmings of Pretty's represented the Foxash and Newbourne tenants and also co-ordinated litigation on behalf of all the firms involved.

It was a long slog. But seven years later, the ministry settled out of court, two months or so before the scheduled hearing. The *East Anglian Daily Times* on 28th August 1991 carried a photo with the caption *"Dick Hemmings of Pretty's, hands the cheque for £6,490,000 to John Harris, corporate banking manager of the Midland Bank, Ipswich."*

Payouts ranged between £10,000 and £55,000. Mr Hemmings was reported as saying that *"The ministry's offer was met with mixed feelings. A number were pleased with the terms, others thought the figures were derisory."* The paper also noted that *"The settlement is a personal victory for Mr Nicholas Packer, 45, who runs a 12-acre smallholding at Newbourne, near Woodbridge, Suffolk, the first grower to seek a legal challenge against what he felt was the mismanagement of the association."*

Today the LSA Charitable Trust draws upon its modest residual assets to support objectives connected with the association's original purpose in production horticulture and co-operative rural enterprise. This includes supporting former tenants and employees who have faced financial hardship.

RESERVATIONS

In his 2005 paper, Philip Hamlett disputed the accuracy of figures given in the CCAHC report in 1980, and consequently challenged the report's conclusions. He wrote that its basic errors and inaccurate comparisons *"made the conclusions quite meaningless. The report was not accepted but remained unchallenged in detail at the time.* This inevitably led him to dismiss the synopsis of another expert witness, submitted in connection with the pending court case, for including *"fanciful estimates of supposed higher profits which should have resulted for the LSA growers based on the inaccurate figures in the CCHAC report."*

Other reports were assessed by Hamlett. Several, totalling over 1,100 pages, were by a professional expert witness whose figures *"gave cause for considerable doubt as to his methods and conclusions."* He concludes, *"With his level of overkill, he was certainly risking a very uncomfortable time in the witness box."* A forensic accountant introduced into the litigation was *"obviously a very trusting soul. His forensic abilities should have led him to question much of the* [expert witness's] *working."*

Hamlett concluded that readers of his comments *"will be rather puzzled that an out-of-court settlement was reached between apparently determined litigants and MAFF, which was faced with a case which could certainly have been opposed."* He suggested two reasons for this turn of events.

First, he had evidence that the litigants' representatives had long regarded a settlement as a preferable conclusion. Second, the ministry expected that the case, if it went ahead, would have lasted at least three months, at a cost of over £4 million to the public purse.

Eventually, MAAF offered £6.5 million, which included interest, and agreed to waive the small number of debts still owed by the plaintiffs. There was no admission of liability.

The offer was accepted, rather to the surprise of many on the legal side of MAAF, said Hamlett. He himself was not surprised, sensing that there was little heart among tenants for a protracted fight.

The settlement left non-litigants with nothing. They had made no claims, but the omission of any acknowledgement of their position did cause some uproar at the time.

Hamlett concluded: *"My own lasting regret is that the out-of-court settlement, though made without liability, still left unchallenged the many unjustified and in some cases quite inaccurate claims against the services provided on the estates."*

POSTSCRIPT

It is important to stress that the Land Settlement Association was not a failure. My father was able to provide for himself and his family for 27 years as an LSA smallholder. Wally Hammond said that, *"some of us made a good living out of it."* Many others would have agreed with him.

The association did achieve its original objective in enabling many long-term unemployed men to establish themselves as successful growers. Those objectives had to change when war was declared, and as a result provided many others with a first step on the agricultural ladder. As Mike Perry of the Plunkett Foundation points out, *"Too often farming and horticulture is about a small number of highly paid people with high skills, using low paid, low skilled labour. LSA-ers were well trained and good growers. This will have impacted upon their work satisfaction."*

The LSA increasingly focused on highly skilled growing, and pioneered new products like bagged salad, cherry tomatoes and little gem lettuce in the UK market. They also pioneered new processes – for example, growing under cloches in the early days, and later, cold chain processes whereby the shelf life of products is extended by an uninterrupted series of storage and distribution activities maintained within a given temperature range.

For almost 50 years the scheme had provided opportunities in horticulture and agriculture for numerous men, as well as providing high quality salad produce for the nation's tables. As I wrote in my Preface, just before its official winding up, the LSA was described in parliament as *"the largest producer of salad crops in Britain."*

It is clear to me that the Land Settlement Association's eventual demise was the consequence of structural weaknesses, and one cannot help but wonder what might have been, had the inherent contradictions within the set-up been addressed. Mike Perry affirms that *"the issue of 'compulsory co-operative' is absolutely key. A co-operative is a member-owned ... body controlled on the basis of one member, one vote. Those benefiting from the co-operative control it. Critically, participating in a co-operative should be voluntary – compulsory co-operation isn't true co-operation. Margaret Digby, the global expert on farmer co-operatives from the 1930s to 1980, called a number of times for independent estates that were organised as true co-operatives."*

If Margaret Digby had been listened to, perhaps the LSA would still be the largest producer of salad crops in Britain.

But then hindsight is a wonderful thing.

SOURCES

Land settlers go back to slum homes, Cairns Post, July 5th 1938

Unemployed! Industrial transfers, Picture Post, February 11th 1939

From dole to farm, The Times, May 8th 1939

The Newbourn Estate, The Field, Ralph Whitlock, June 14th 1947

An experiment in smallholdings Land Settlement Assoc'n, ca 1949

Farming costs shared, The Field, Ralph Whitlock, April 17th 1958

The Newbourn Settlement, The East Anglian Magazine, Walter Tye, March 1961

The Land Settlement Association – Its History and Present Form K J McCready. Occasional Paper 37, Plunkett F'ndation, 1974.

Time-proven, but adaptable, Country Life, Sept 10th 1981

Hansard, 20th December 1982: Stanley Newens, MP for Harlow

Swords into ploughshares and back, manuscript of an unpublished book by Richard "Dick" Whittaker, 1984, used by kind permission of his daughter, Sue Whittaker.

Village life in and around Felixstowe, Smith, Wylie, White & Hadwen, 2003

The Land Settlement Association Ltd, 1934 – 1983: An epilogue, Philip G Hamlett, 2005

'Go home, you miners!': Fen Drayton and the LSA, Pamela Dearlove, 2007 (£8.95 from Pamela at redtiles@mac.com)

The Land Settlement Association: Its co-operative ideals and their implementation, Peter Clarke, Northampton Sq, *2012*

The national archives of the Land Settlement Association are held at the Museum of English Rural Life, University of Reading, Redlands Road, Reading RG1 5EX. Some archive material is also held by the Plunkett Foundation, The Quadrangle, Woodstock OX20 1LH